# Crochet Patterns 2in 1

The Ultimate Beginner's Guide To learn Crochet and create Any Design You Want with Easy-to-Follow Illustration Patterns.

By

Eleanor Patel

© Copyright 2021 - All rights reserved.

This document is geared towards providing exact and reliable information in regards to the topic and issue covered. The publication is sold with the idea that the publisher is not required to render accounting, officially permitted, or otherwise, qualified services. If advice is necessary, legal or professional, a practiced individual in the profession should be ordered.

- From a Declaration of Principles which was accepted and approved equally by a Committee of the American Bar Association and a Committee of Publishers and Associations.

In no way is it legal to reproduce, duplicate, or transmit any part of this document in either electronic means or in printed format. Recording of this publication is strictly prohibited, and any storage of this document is not allowed unless with written permission from the publisher. All rights reserved.

The information provided herein is stated to be truthful and consistent, in that any liability, in terms of inattention or otherwise, by any usage or abuse of any policies, processes, or Instructions: contained within is the solitary and utter responsibility of the recipient reader. Under no circumstances will any legal responsibility or blame be held against the publisher for any reparation, damages, or monetary loss due to the information herein, either directly or indirectly.

Respective authors own all copyrights not held by the publisher.

The information herein is offered for informational purposes solely and is universal as so. The presentation of the information is without contract or any type of guarantee assurance.

The trademarks that are used are without any consent, and the publication of the trademark is without permission or backing by the trademark owner. All trademarks and brands within this book are for clarifying purposes only and are owned by the owners themselves, not affiliated with this document.

# Table of Content

| | |
|---|---|
| **Book One** | **10** |
| **Crochet For Beginners** | **10** |
| **Introduction** | **12** |
| **Chapter 1: What is Crochet & its Basics** | **14** |
| *1.1 Crochet by Tambour* | *15* |
| *1.2 Crochet by Irish Famine* | *16* |
| *1.3 Items Yielded by Crochet* | *18* |
| *1.4 Yesterday & Today's Techniques* | *19* |
| *1.5 Patterns* | *20* |
| **Chapter 2: Crocheting Tools** | **23** |
| *2.1 Crochet Hook* | *23* |
| *2.2 Measuring Tools* | *23* |
| *2.3 Scissors* | *24* |
| *2.4 Tapestry Needle* | *25* |
| *2.5 Yarn & Gauge* | *25* |
| **Chapter 3: Techniques for Crocheting** | **28** |
| *3.1 Crochet Hooks* | *28* |
| *3.2 Holding a Crochet Hook* | *28* |
| *3.3 Making a Slip Knot* | *29* |
| *3.4 Crocheting a Chain Stitch* | *29* |
| *3.5 Single Crochet* | *29* |
| *3.6 Single Crochet Stitch Patterns* | *30* |
| *3.7 Double Crochet* | *30* |
| *3.8 Crochet a Granny Square* | *30* |
| *3.9 Make a Slip Stitch* | *31* |
| *3.10 Working the Basic Crochet Stitches* | *31* |
| *3.11 Finished Crochet* | *31* |

 3.12 Learning Crochet Left-Handed   31

 3.13 Check the Tension   32

 3.14 Following a Pattern   33

## Conclusion   67

## Book Two   69

## CROCHET   69

## Introduction   71

## Chapter: 1 Introduction to Crochet   73

## Chapter: 2 Tools and Requirements   76

 1. Crochet hook   76

 2. Yarn   76

 3. Darning needle   77

 4. Scissors   77

 5. Hook organizer   77

 6. Stitch Markers   77

 7. Measurement tape   78

 8. Stitch Patterns   78

 9. Crochet Book   78

 10. Row Counter   79

 11. Crochet Materials Organizer   79

 12. Aluminum & Plastic   79

## Chapter: 3 Types of Crochet   80

 1. Crochet type one (amigurumi style)   80

 2. Crochet type two (Bavarian)   81

 4. Crochet type four (Bullion)   82

 5. Crochet type five (Broomstick)   82

 6. Crochet type six (Aran)   83

 7. Crochet type seven (clothesline)   83

 8. Crochet type eight (Bosnian)   84

9. Crochet type nine (Clones Lace) ................................. 84
10. Crochet type ten (Tunisian) .................................... 85
11. Crochet type eleven (Filet) ..................................... 86
12. Crochet type twelve (Hairpin) .................................. 87
13. Crochet type thirteen (finger) .................................. 87
14. Crochet type fourteen (Microns) ............................... 88
15. Crochet type fifteen (freeform) ................................ 89
16. Crochet type sixteen (Pineapple) .............................. 89
17. Crochet type seventeen (symbol) .............................. 90
18. Crochet type eighteen (overlay) ............................... 90

## Chapter: 4 Techniques For Using Crochet .......... 92

1. Crochet technique one (Front and Back Loop Single Crochet) ... 92
2. Crochet technique two (Magic Circle) ......................... 92
3. Crochet technique three (Loop HDC) .......................... 93
4. Crochet technique four (Crab stitch) .......................... 93
5. Crochet technique five (Foundation) ........................... 94
6. Crochet technique six (Standing Stitches) ..................... 95
7. Crochet technique seven (Shells stitches) ..................... 95

## Different Knitting Techniques .......... 95

1. Knitting technique one (Combination Knitting) ................ 95
2. Knitting technique two (Through the Back Loop) .............. 96
3. Knitting technique three (Brioche) ............................ 96

## Specialized Crochet and knitting methods. .......... 97

1. Method one (Tunisian Crochet) ................................. 97
2. Method two (Crochet Colorwork) ............................... 97
3. Method three (C2C crochet) .................................... 98
4. Method four (Knitting entrelac) ................................ 98
5. Method five (Cables) ........................................... 98
6. Method six (fair isle) ........................................... 99
7. Method seven (Mosaic Knitting) ................................ 99

### Chapter: 5 Crochet projects, home Products and gifts — 100

*1. Infinity Scarf* — *100*
*2. Tape Measure* — *101*
*3. Crochet Baby Cardigan* — *101*
*4. Crochet Necklace* — *101*
*5. Grocery Bag* — *102*
*6. Chain Necklace* — *102*
*7. Hot Pad* — *103*
*8. Hook Case* — *103*
*9. Pencil Holder* — *103*
*10. Yarn Holder* — *104*
*11. Headband* — *104*
*12. Dishcloth* — *105*
*13. Baby Blanket* — *106*
*14. Ear Bud Covers* — *106*
*15. Slippers* — *107*
*16. Stuff Unicorn* — *108*
*17. Massage Soap Saver* — *108*
*18. Mug Cover* — *109*
*19. Crochet Coasters* — *110*
*20. Stitch Markers* — *110*
*21. Laptop Cover* — *110*

### Chapter: 6 Crocheted Socks and Gloves and mittens — 112

### Socks Patterns — 112

*1. Pattern one (Ribbed Pattern)* — *112*
*2. Pattern two (free pattern)* — *112*
*3. Pattern three (Nicole Cormier)* — *113*
*4. Pattern four (Ball Hank n Skein)* — *113*
*5. Pattern five (Crochet Ankle Socks)* — *113*
*6. Pattern six (Step-by-Step Crochet Socks Pattern)* — *114*

| | |
|---|---:|
| 7. Pattern seven (Slipper Socks Pattern) | *114* |
| 8. Pattern eight (Cabled socks Pattern) | *114* |

## Handwear crochet products     **116**

| | |
|---|---:|
| 1. Fingerless Mittens | *116* |
| 2. Adult Sized Mittens | *117* |
| 3. Button Cuff Mittens | *117* |
| 4. Fingerless Gloves | *117* |
| 5. Frozen Fingers Mittens | *118* |
| 6. Flip-Top Mittens | *119* |
| 7. Hybrid Mittens | *120* |
| 8. Twine Knit Mitts | *121* |
| 9. Colorful Mittens | *121* |
| 10. iPhone Mitts | *122* |
| 11. Matrix Mittens | *122* |
| 12. Shark Mittens | *123* |
| 13. Adult Newfie Mitten | *124* |
| 14. Retro Crocheted Mittens | *124* |
| 15. Puff Crochet Mittens | *124* |
| 16. Snowfall Mittens | *125* |
| 17. Squirrel Mittens | *125* |

## Chapter: 7 Hats and Scarves     **127**

## Hats Designs     **127**

| | |
|---|---:|
| *Easy Crochet Hat Patterns for Beginners* | *127* |
| 1. Design one (Simple Crochet Beanie) | *127* |
| 2. Design two (Leigh Textured Crochet Hat) | *128* |
| 3. Design three (simple Crochet Beanie) | *129* |

## Scarf styles     **130**

| | |
|---|---:|
| 1. Style one (Striped Neck Scarf) | *130* |
| 2. Style two (Infinity Scarf) | *130* |
| 3. Style three (Textured Scarf) | *131* |

    4. Style four (Chunky Crochet Scarf)      132

    5. Style five (Super Scarf)      132

    6. Style six (Ribbed Scarf)      132

    7. Style seven (The Boyfriend Scarf)      133

    8. Style eight (Simple Scarf)      134

    9. Style nine (Double Crochet Scarf)      134

    10. Style eleven (Reeva Scarf)      134

    11. Style eleven (Basic Scarf)      134

**Chapter: 8 Crochet Bags**      **136**

    1. Bag pattern one (Market Bag Pattern)      136

    2. Bag pattern two (Yarn Bag Pattern)      136

    3. Bag pattern three (Tote Pattern)      137

    4. Bag pattern four (Free Crochet Bag Pattern)      137

    5. Bag pattern five (Granny Bag Pattern)      137

    6. Bag pattern six (Summer Bag Pattern)      138

    7. Bag pattern seven (Market Tote Pattern)      139

    8. Bag pattern eight (Market Bag Pattern)      139

    9. Bag pattern nine (Fancy Bag Pattern)      139

    10. Bag pattern ten (Masa Bag Pattern)      140

    11. Bag pattern eleven (Bag of Colors Pattern)      140

    12. Bag pattern twelve (Mesh Bag Pattern)      140

    13. Bag pattern thirteen (Dot's Bag Pattern)      141

    14. Bag pattern fourteen (The Dragon Egg Bag Pattern)      141

    15. Bag pattern fifteen (Raffia Messenger Bag)      141

    16. Bag pattern sixteen (Kitty Bag Pattern)      142

    17. Bag pattern seventeen (Raffia Bag Pattern)      142

    18. Bag pattern eighteen (Fat Bag Pattern)      142

    19. Bag pattern nineteen (Market Bag Pattern)      142

**Conclusion**      **144**

# Book One

# Crochet For Beginners

The Ultimate Step by Step Guide With Picture illustrations To Learn How to Crochet. Master Your First Project In Less Than 2 Hours and Create Wonderful Projects

By

Eleanor Patel

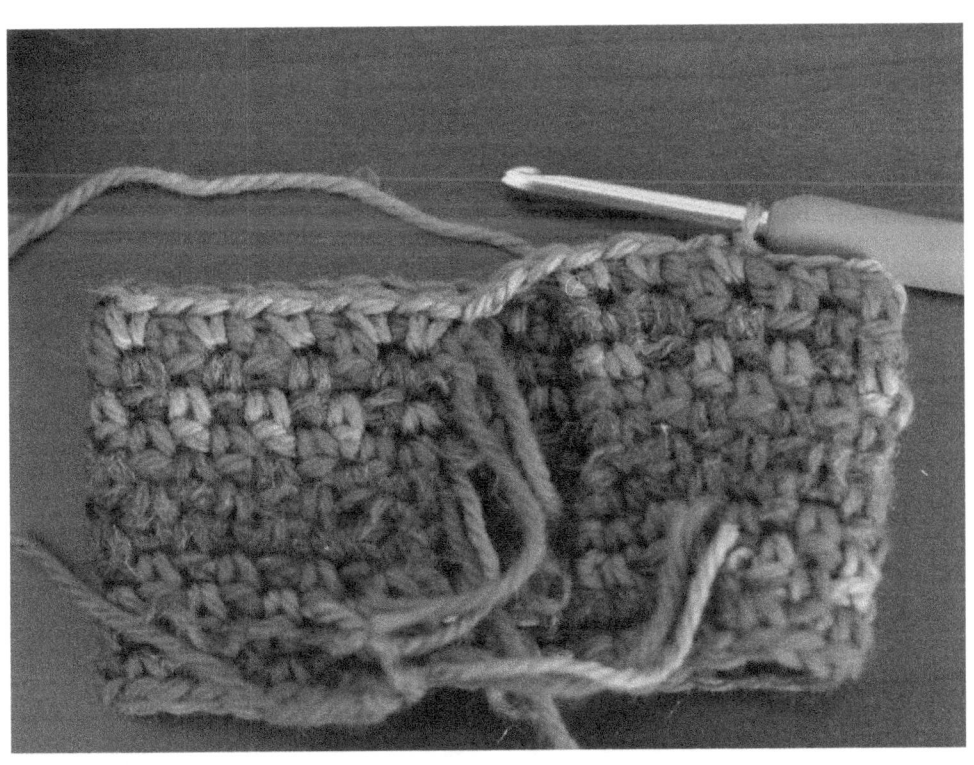

# Introduction

Crochet is a very flexible and popular method, and like knitting, after you master a few fundamental stitches, you can combine them to make amazing clothes and home items. Just you need is some yarn to crochet & a hook. To begin, build a basic loop (you will find it further in the book) to serve as the foundation row for all subsequent rows or rounds. Crochet stitches are formed by wrapping yarn around a hook to form loops. To form the stitches, the loops are dragged through the wrapped yarn. The chain stitches foundation may also be used to produce drawstrings or cords for knitting projects. Crochet may be used to construct both entire garments and attractive edgings for knitting. Lightweight yarns generate a delicate fabric, whereas heavier yarns provide a denser fabric, similar to knitting. Crochet is a simple skill to pick up, & your work will expand rapidly, so you'll be crafting lovely products in no time. Don't be afraid to give it a go.

Weaving, Knitting, netting, twisting, braiding, & knotting are only few of the needlework techniques that have been termed by several names throughout history. knotless netting, Needle-coiling, cross-knit looping, vatsom, looped needle-netting, Coptic knitting, nalbinding, tambour, Tunisian crochet, needle lace, lace creation, tatting, macramé, sprang, and shepherd's knitting is some of the techniques.

Hair, reeds, grasses, animal fur & sinew, hemp, wool, flax, gold and silver strands, wool yarns (soft zephyr yam, white cotton thread, luster yarn, carpet yarn), double cable yarn, cotton yarn (anchor & Estremadura), silk thread (cordonnet & floss), linen thread, mohair, hemp thread, chenille, novelty mixtures, meta

We now have a large assortment of cotton, wool, silk, and synthetic yarns at our disposal. Copper wire, plastic strips, sisal, jute, fabric scraps, unspun wool, & even dog hair are all possibilities for crocheting.

What about the crochet needle? Today, we may acquire plastic, aluminum, or steel hooks in moreover 25 sizes from a yarn store or Walmart. They utilized anything they could get their hands on in the past, including fingers, metal hooks, wood, animal bone, fishbone, horn, old spoons, comb teeth, brass, morse (walrus tusk), tortoiseshell, mother-of-pearl, ivory, copper, vulcanite, steel, ebonite, silver, and agate.

# Chapter 1: What is Crochet & its Basics

Crochet is a term used by the French, Belgians, Italians, and Spanish-speaking people. In Holland, the skill was known as haken, in Denmark as haekling, in Norway as hekling, and in Sweden as virkning.

Knitting, needlework, and weaving, for example, may be traced back in time owing to archaeological findings, literary sources, and diverse graphical depictions. However, no one knows exactly when or where the crochet began. The name derives from the Center French word croc, or croche, which means hook, & the Old Norse word krokr, which means hook.

"The modern technique of real crochet as we know it now was established around the 16th century," as per American crochet expert & globe traveler Annie Potter. In France, it was known as 'crochet lace,' while in England, it was known as 'chain lace.' Walter Edmund Roth met relatives of a Guiana Indians in 1916, she says, and saw specimens of real crochet.

Lis Paludan of Denmark, another writer/researcher who focused her hunt for the roots of crochet on Europe, has three intriguing hypotheses. One: Crochet started in Arabia, traveled eastward to Tibet, then west to Spain, from which it spread to other Mediterranean nations through Arab trade routes. Two: The first evidence of crochet was found in South America, where such a primitive culture was claimed to utilize crochet adornments in puberty ceremonies. Three: Early instances of three-dimensional crochet dolls have been found in China.

However, according to Paludan, "no conclusive evidence on how ancient the technique of crochet could be and where it comes from." Crochet was almost unknown in Europe until the year 1800. "Many sources claim that crochet dates back to the 1500s in Italy when it was used by nuns for church linens under the moniker of 'nun's or 'nun's work' lace,'" she explains. Her investigation found up a number of instances of lace-making & a kind of ribbon tape, most of which have been survived, but "all indications suggest that crochet was not recognized in Italy as early as the 16th century"—under any name.

## 1.1 Crochet by Tambour

Crochet is said to have evolved most naturally from Chinese handiwork, a very old kind of embroidery found in Turkey, India, Persia, and North Africa that arrived in Europe in the 1700s & was dubbed "tambouring" from the French word "tambour," which means "drum." A backdrop cloth is stretched tight on a frame in this method. Underneath the cloth, a working thread is retained. A hook-tipped needle is put into the cloth & a loop of a working thread is dragged up through it. A hook then is inserted a little farther along with the loop remaining on it, & another circle of the netting is brought up & worked through the 1st loop to make a chain stitch. The tambour hook was just as tiny as a sewing needle, implying that the job was done with a very fine thread.

Tambour developed into "crochet in the air" around the end of the eighteenth century when the backdrop cloth was removed and the stitch was let to work on its own.

Crochet first appeared in Europe during the early 1800s, and Mlle gave it a huge push. Riego de Branchardiere was most recognized for her ability to convert old-fashioned needle & bobbin lace patterns into crochet patterns that could be readily replicated. She wrote a lot of pattern books enough so millions of ladies could start copying her designs. Madame. Riego also claims to be the inventor of "lace-like" crochet, which is now known as Irish crochet.

## 1.2 Crochet by Irish Famine

For the citizens of Ireland, Irish crochet had been a lifeline. It rescued them from a potato famine that lasted from 1845-1850 & plunged them into destitution.

The Irish had difficult living and working circumstances during this period. To take full advantage of the sunshine, they knitted in between agricultural tasks and outside. They went inside after dark to work by candlelight, a slow-burning peat fire, or an oil lamp.

Because many of them were living in filth, finding a place to store their crochet work was a challenge. If they didn't have somewhere else to put it, it went beneath the bed, where it eventually got filthy. Fortunately, the crocheted item could be cleaned and restored to its former brilliance. Ironically, purchasers in other countries were unaware that such fine collars & cuffs were produced in shacks in impoverished areas.

Crochet cooperatives were formed in Ireland, bringing together men, women, and children. Schools were established to teach the trade, and instructors were educated and sent across Ireland, where workers quickly developed their own designs. Despite the fact that over a million people perished in less than ten years, the people of Irish managed to endure the famine. Crochet earnings enabled families to save enough money to move & make a fresh start in another country, bringing their crochet abilities with them. According to Potter, two million Irish people moved to America between 1845 & 1859, and four million in 1900. American women, preoccupied with spinning, weaving, knitting, and quilting, couldn't help but be encouraged to include the crochet talents of their new neighbors into their handiwork.

a stiff wire or A needle, put into a piece of wood or tree bark or a cork, with its end filed down & curved into a small hook, was what at least one individual in Ireland used to manufacture excellent Irish crochet during the Great Famine (1845-1850).

## 1.3 Items Yielded by Crochet

Men - because it was their profession - developed handwork for utilitarian needs in the early ages. To capture animals and capture fish or birds, hunters and fishermen used knotted strands of ropes, woven fibers, or strips of fabric. Knotted fishing nets, game bags, and open-worked cooking utensils were among the other applications.

Personal ornamentation for special events such as religious ceremonies, festivities, weddings, and funerals was added to handwork. Ceremonial dresses may have crocheted embellishment and ornate trims on the arms, ankles, and wrists.

Royalty and the affluent in sixteenth-century Europe showered themselves in lace - trimmings, dresses, coats, and headpieces - whereas the common people could only dream of donning such garments. Crochet is said to have evolved as a poor man's copy of the wealthy man's lace.

Crochet patterns for birdcage covers, flowerpot holders, baskets for lamp mats, visiting cards, and wastepaper baskets, tablecloths, shades, antimacassars (or "antis," tends to cover to prevent chairbacks from the hair oil used by men in the middle of the 1800s), purses, tobacco pouches, men's caps & waistcoats, and even a rug with foot warmers to be placed undecorated were available in Victorian times.

Women crocheted Afghans, sleeping rugs, traveling rugs, sleigh rugs, chaise lounge rugs, vehicle rugs, cushions, coffee, and teapot cozies, & hot-water bottle covers between 1900 and 1930. Potholders first appeared about this period and quickly became a mainstay of the crocheter's repertory.

Of course, now you can do anything you want. Crochet became popular in the 1960s and 1970s as a freeform form of expression that can now be seen in three-dimensional sculptures, clothes, carpets, and tapestries depicting abstract and realistic motifs and settings.

## 1.4 Yesterday & Today's Techniques

It's fascinating to compare and contrast old and new crochet techniques. For example, from 1824 to 1833, the Dutch periodical Penelope noted that both yarn & the hooks were to be kept in the right hand, with the yarn being transferred over the hooks from the proper forefinger. The hook is handled within the right hand & the yarn inside the left in crochet book from the 1840s, much as right-handers use today.

It was mentioned in a German article from 1847 that one must "Keep the tension consistent, either loosely or securely crocheted; otherwise, an appealingly even texture would not be obtained. Furthermore, if you are not crocheting in a round, you must break off the yarn at the last of each row to give the crocheted item a finer finish." Thankfully, today's designs frequently teach us to work on both the right & wrong sides of the cloth we're working with. This shift occurred at the switch off the century.

The injunction to preserve the very same tension "does seem to imply the crochet hooks were from the same thickness & that the crocheter was required to work in the right tension as per the design," according to researcher Lis Paludan.

Old pattern instructions from the mid-1800s said that the hook should only be put into the rear half of the stitch and that a single crochet stitch should be used unless otherwise specified. In 1847, a European, Jenny Lambert, noted that putting the single crochet hook into the rear half of the stitch was good for producing table runners and other items, but entering the hooks through both loops can be used "for crochet sole for shoes & other products which must be thicker than usual, but the method is not suited for patterns." Unless otherwise instructed, we now automatically cycle through both loops.

## 1.5 Patterns

Before patterns were actually written, people would just copy the work of others. Samples were sewed onto pages in scrapbooks, sewed onto huge pieces of cloth, or stored loose in a box or bag. Author Annie Potter discovered several of these scrapbooks, which date from the late 1800s, still being used by nuns in Spain during her travels.

Crocheting various stitches together within long, thin bands - some created by adults, others started in school & added to overtime - was another method to gather stitch samples. (From 1916 until roughly 1926 in Europe, readers could purchase miniature pattern samples together with their yarn.)

The first recorded crochet designs were published in 1824.

The first colorwork crochet handbag designs were for gold & silver silk thread handbags.

Crochet books could be obtained in a variety of nations, and they were often translated through one language to another. Riego de la Branchardiere was the most well-known crochet specialist, having written over a hundred books, many of which were on crochet.

Crochet books first from the mid-nineteenth century were tiny, measuring around 4 inches to 6 inches, but they had woodcut pictures. Paludan informs us that these little gems included designs for cuffs, white lace-like collars, lace, insertions, and caps for ladies and children, as well as handbag designs for men's slippers and hats. Spool yarn (Scottish thread on spools), Cotton thread, linen, or hemp thread were advised for white crochet (insertions, matting, edgings, underwear trimming). Silk, chenille yarns &, wool, as well as gold & silver threads, were recommended for colorwork.

Modern crocheters would be enraged by those early designs, which were often inaccurate. For example, an eight-pointed star might turn out to have just six points. The reader was supposed to study the pattern yet utilize the graphic as a more precise guide, it turns out.

# Chapter 2: Crocheting Tools

Crocheting requires the use of certain tools. Before you purchase, do some research on the tools to ensure you get decent equipment.

## 2.1 Crochet Hook

The first instrument needed is a crochet hook. Crochet designs specify the hook size to be used. This book will assist you in selecting hooks for your 1st project.

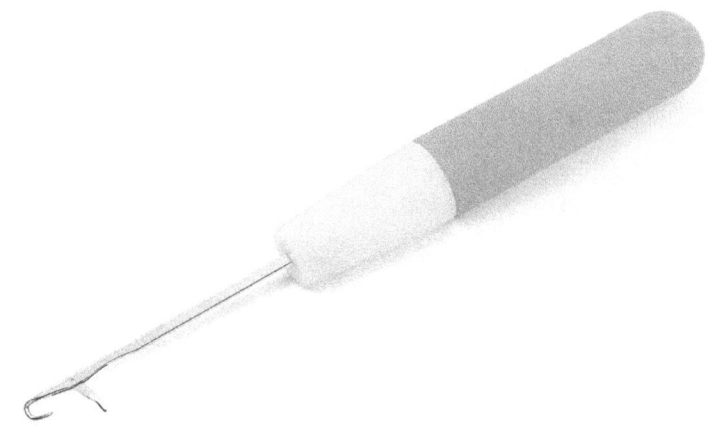

## 2.2 Measuring Tools

You'll need a ruler, a metal-measuring gauge, or a measuring tape to do the measurements.

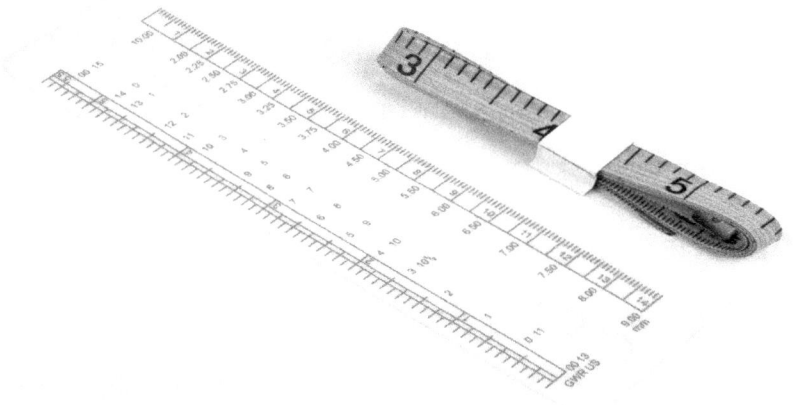

## 2.3 Scissors

Cut yarn, trim pompoms, and so on using shears or a tiny pair of scissors. To keep scissors safe, store them in a case.

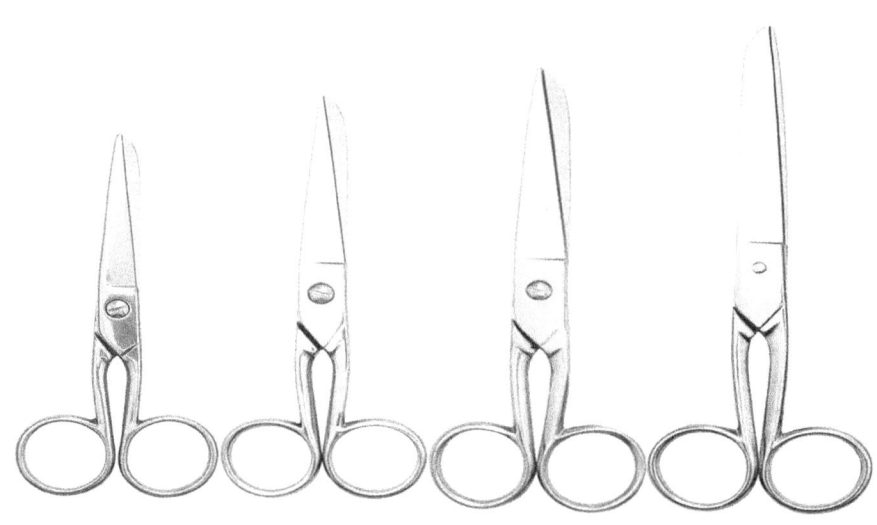

## 2.4 Tapestry Needle

Seams are sewn using a tapestry needle with a blunt tip. The ideal needle is a steel needle that is straight.

Around the eye of certain tapestry needles is a "hump." They're not suitable for crocheting seams since the hump snags on stitches & makes pulling the yarn through difficult.

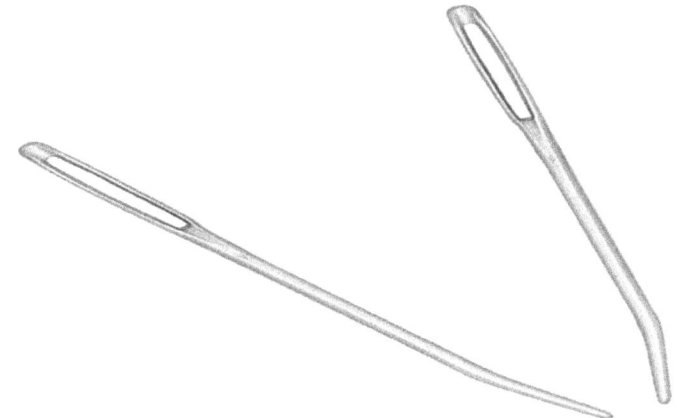

## 2.5 Yarn & Gauge

**Yarn**

Yarns come in various weights (the thickness of said strands) & fiber compositions.

Use the yarn recommended in the instructions for best results. Make careful to buy all of the yarn you'll need for the project at once since dye lots might differ slightly in shade, which will show up in the completed product. If you're working with many varieties of yarn in the same project, ensure sure they're all washed in the same way. Care instructions may be found upon the product label; carefully follow them. Always create a swatch before measuring the gauge.

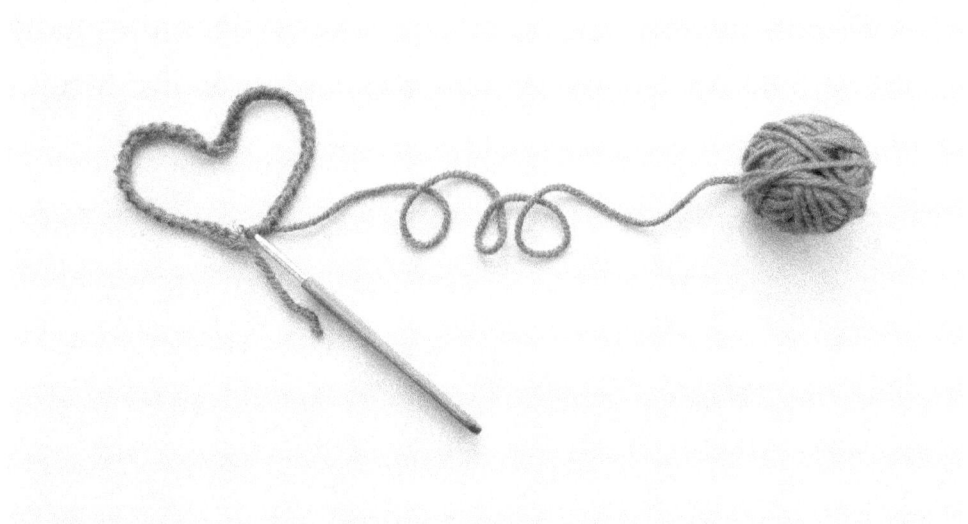

**Gauge**

The numbers of stitches (& spaces) per inch, as well as the rows (rounds) per inch, are known as gauges. Gauge is stated over 4 inches in several designs. In order for your item to be the proper size, your gauge & the gauge indicated in the pattern should be the same. This is particularly important when working on projects which must fit together. Take your time to produce a gauge swatch before you begin your project. Use the same yarn, hook, and pattern stitch as in the instructions to verify the gauge. Make a 6-inch square swatch out of the fabric. Knit for approximately 6 inches in the pattern, then bind off. Allow the swatch to settle for a few moments before flattening it and measuring it. Mark off a piece of stitches measuring 4 inches square in the middle of the swatch using pins. In this 4 inch portion, count the amount of stitches and rows. If you match the gauges, you may begin working on your design straight away. You're knitting too loosely if you do have too few stitches; switch to a smaller hook and produce another swatch. You're working too tightly if you already have too many stitches; switch to a bigger hook. Continue to make swatches and experiment with hooks sizes until you get the desired gauge. Because everyone crochets differently, you'll be able to find a project that works for you. The yarn size and appropriate hook are listed on the label of each skein of yarn. You should preserve the label for future reference.

Crochet is also done using threads. Crochet thread is often used to make doilies, tablecloths, table toppers, and project edges. A number 10 sized thread is the most widely used thread. The fine the thread, the higher the thread number; so, 20 is better than 10, & 30 is better than 20. For this sort of crocheting, you'll need a threading hook. With such a size 10 thread, a "0" hook works perfectly.

# Chapter 3: Techniques for Crocheting

Crocheting is a delicate technique that can be used to produce wonderful presents for others as well as things for your home & wardrobe. Begin by learning a few fundamental stitches, then progress to more complex basic stitches. To begin, choose the size and kind of hook that is most suitable for you. Then begin with basic yarns and basic designs, and you'll be an expert in no time.

## 3.1 Crochet Hooks

Crochet doesn't need a lot of materials to get started. The crochet hook is the most important component, and there are many various sizes and varieties available. If you're looking for a novice crochet hook, use one made of aluminum since the yarn will glide effortlessly. The following are the 3 basic crochet materials you'll need:

- A size H-8 or I-9 metal crochet hook, whatever feels best on your hand
- A wool yarn or ball of acrylic or skein
- Scissors

## 3.2 Holding a Crochet Hook

Begin by gripping your crochet hook in the same way you would a pencil, using your thumb & index finger gripping the hook at the finger hold in the center. For more comfort and control, slip your middle finger up it toward the hook's tip.

The hook will be slightly angled towards you, but not downward or upward.

## 3.3 Making a Slip Knot

One of the first things you'll need to learn to crochet is how to tie a slips knot onto the crochet hook. It's how you'll thread the yarn onto the hook and begin crocheting. Loop & Twist the yarn onto the hook as quickly as possible, then wrap it around the hook and draw that through the loop to tightening it. Do not worry if it seems weird at first; with practice, it will get easier.

## 3.4 Crocheting a Chain Stitch

The chain stitch is frequently the first stitch learned by new crocheters. Because chain stitches are the basis of most crochet items, they are among the most essential fundamental stitches to master. The shorthand for the chain stitches in a design is "ch," or "chs" for such plural form. The letter "ch" is generally associated with a number. For example, ch 135 indicates that 135 chain stitches should be crocheted.

## 3.5 Single Crochet

You'll learn the important single crochet stitch once you've mastered the chain stitch. The single crochet stitching can generally be abbreviated as "sc" in a design, along with the amount of stitches you will need to create.

## 3.6 Single Crochet Stitch Patterns

You are prepared to undertake a starting project now that you understand how to tie a slip knot & basic stitches. You might begin by crocheting a scarf or a baby blanket for beginners. For the sake of simplicity, several introductory patterns may also be written without abbreviations. Take your time and be gentle with yourself as you start your first endeavor. It's ok if you have to restart the pattern from the beginning if necessary.

## 3.7 Double Crochet

By mastering the double crochet stitch, you may take your crochet skills to the next level. When you master this stitch, you will be able to make Afghan granny squares. Make little swatches till your doubled crochet stitches are consistent. A double crochet stitch is abbreviated as "dc" plus the amount of the double crochet stitches provided in the design.

## 3.8 Crochet a Granny Square

A granny square is made out of a cluster of double crochet stitches. From blanket to pillow covers, the granny squares are the core of a crocheted items, & you can even sew these together to make a warm and snug doggy sweater. Make them one color or multicolored, but whichever color scheme you choose, know that with each square you make, you're improving as a crocheter.

## 3.9 Make a Slip Stitch

In crochet, slip stitches are useful for a variety of things. They may be used to link pieces together, make basic completed edges, and add a decorative element to a crocheted piece's surface. You may also use the stitches in rows to make a thick material. Bosnian Crochet is a technique for crocheting a cloth using the slip stitch (or often a variety of further names).

## 3.10 Working the Basic Crochet Stitches

Learn additional fundamental crochet stitches, such as the half double stitch, which generates a herringbone pattern, the treble (or triple crochet stitch), which generates a higher thread, & the Tunisian crochet stitch, which may mimic a knit fabric.

## 3.11 Finished Crochet

Crochet finishing methods are an essential aspect of the craft. You'll need to know how to produce broad and narrow edgings in addition to the slip stitch, which provides basic edging. A single crochet stitch is the simplest way to make an edge. Even with rounded corners, it's a fantastic option.

## 3.12 Learning Crochet Left-Handed

You may crochet with your left hand as well. Traditional crochet designs were intended primarily for right-handed crocheters, but so many modern designs also contain instructions for left-handed craftspeople. You'll discover lots of tips and methods to aid you along the road, & most importantly, you'll meet and learn from a lot of other lefty crocheters.

## 3.13 Check the Tension

Crocheting a certain size is determined by the hook size, yarn, stitch design, and you. Crochet designs provide the stitch, number of stitches, and rows necessary at the outset. Because no two individuals have the same tension, construct a trial swatch of at least 6x6 inches (15x15 cm) before beginning a project to confirm your tension matches the patterns. Your tension is too slack, and you'll need to switch to a smaller hook if your swatch has fewer stitches & rows. If you have too many, tension is too slack, and you should switch to a larger hook. Before you begin, try another sample and keep in mind that matching the numbers of stitches is typically more essential than matching the number of rows, since you may adjust for rows with working more or less to the pattern's specifications.

- Place a ruler or stiff tape all across the sample at the end of a row of stitches to measure your stitches. Place two pins 4 inches (10 cm) apart & count the stitches between them.
- Place the rulers or tapes along a column of stitches to determine row tension. Insert two pins 4 inches (10cm) apart, avoiding the edges, then count the rows in between pins.

## 3.14 Following a Pattern

Crochet designs are written in condensed form, similar to knitting patterns. Here's how to figure out when, where, and why to do something.

Read over the pattern before you start crocheting to make sure you know what should do in every section.

- At the conclusion of each circle, don't turn in the work.
- The turning chain is always counted as a stitch.
- In the preceding row, work into the next available stitch.
- Unless it's a loop or chain stitch, always put the hook beneath the upper loops of a stitch.
- In a pattern, the order to work 'even' implies to work without growing or decreasing.
- Asterisks are being used to indicate when a pattern is repeated in a row.
- A stitch combination is enclosed in brackets or parentheses and would be repeated in the direction indicated.

# Chapter 4: Projects

## 4.1 Easy Crochet Scarf Pattern Using Moss Stitch

Skill: Beginner, Time: 240 Mins

The moss stitch, that is a simple stitch pattern made up of single crochet & chain stitches, is used in this simple crochet scarf design. Making single crochet threads into gaps formed by chain stitches creates the moss stitch, usually known as linen stitch or granite stitch. It just takes a few rows to master this method, which results in a lovely contemplative pattern that is perfect for beginner and experienced crochets. It's also simple enough for novices, with no rising or decreasing required. This crochet scarf design is a great way to learn and practice this lovely stitch while also making a useful and pleasant item.

**Finished Measurements / Sizing**

4 inches in width

Approximately 50 inches in length

Crochet scarves available in a variety of widths, so it's ok if yours is wider or narrower than the 4-inch average. If you really like the width you've achieved, no need to start again, given you purchased enough yarn. If your scarf is much fuller than 4", the most immediate thing you would have to worry about is running out of yarn.

A crochet scarf's length is easily adjustable. Do you prefer a shorter scarf? Reduce the number of rows you crochet. Is it possible to get a longer scarf? Crochet a few extra rows as long as we have yarn.

**Gauge**

In Moss Stitch, 14 stitches and 15 rows equal 4 inches (10 cm).

Crochet seven to ten rows of the design and measure the breadth of the item to determine your stitch gauge. Compare the initial measurement to the final measurement. If your scarf is turned out to be broader than the measurement provided, you may wish to start afresh with such a smaller crochet hook. If it's becoming too thin, you may want to start anew with a bigger crochet hook.

**Abbreviations**

- ch-1 sp: chain-1 space
- ch: chain
- sc: single crochet
- rep: repeat
- tch: turning chain
- st: stitch
- [ ]: repeat directives within brackets as commanded

**Notes:**

You will be crocheting into chains spaces in this design, which are denoted as ch-1 sp throughout the design. For temporally marking the stitch in this design, use a stitch marker, safety pin, or similar item.

**What You'll Require**

## Tools / Equipment

- Crochet hook, US K/10.5 (6.5 mm)
- Coilless safety pins or stitch markers
- A yarn needle or a tapestry needle
- Scissors

## Materials

- Worsted weight yarn (250-300 yards)

## Instructions

### 1. Create a chain

Make a slip knot & put on the hook, leaving a six-inch tail of yarn; ch 15.

### 2. Work into Chain

In the 1st ch from your hook, place a stitch marker. [Ch 1, skipping upcoming ch, sc in upcoming ch] 6 times; turn. There will be 14 stitches total, with 7 sc stitches and 7 chain gaps (counting the space beside the highlighted stitch).

### Tip

The turning chain was a stitch that is done in the middle of a row of crochet stitches. It elevates the piece's height from the ongoing row to the height required for the following row. It may be taken at the end of the row or at the beginning of a row in patterns. The start of a row may be identified in this design.

### 3. Establish a Foundation Row

**Next Row:** ch 1 (turning chains), [sc in next ch-1 sp & ch 1] 6 times, work sc into ch st at which marker was inserted, removing the marker before working the stitch. Turn around.

## Tip

If you're having trouble locating your ch-1 spaces, gently poke the rows of stitches through the back to the front with your finger, exploring your ways into the work until you get the hang of recognizing where they are.

## 4. Begin with the Moss Stitch.

The remainder of the rows are identical to the previous row, with one slight

exception: at the conclusion of the row, work your final sc into the previous row's turning chain (tch).

**All Rows:** ch 1 (tch), [sc in next chain-1 sp, ch 1] 6 times, work a single crochet into turning chain.

Repeat this row until the scarf is about 50 inches long, or the desired length.

## Finish:

Finish by fastening off, allowing enough yarn to weave in the ends. Use the end of the yarn, thread your tapestries needle & weave it into the design so that it is hidden. Repeat with any additional stray threads you may have. That's all there is to it; now put a crochet scarf around your neck & enjoy it.

## 4.2 Crochet Baby Blanket Pattern

Beginner skill, 300 minute

Who wouldn't want to make a quick and cuddly baby blanket with a free crocheted baby blanket pattern? Do you like fast tasks as much as we do?

You'll be able to finish this beauty in just 5 hours if you use thick yarn & a rapid stitch. This isn't your typical Moss stitch, however. Have you noticed the texture? This blanket was made using extended single crochet stitches, which you will really like.

**Materials:**

- Chenille yarn, size 6, very bulky. The example blanket was made using Bernat Blanket yarn in Dark Grey, Vintage White, & Bernat Baby Blanket in Shell Pink.
- Hook size N/P(10mm)
- To weave within ends, use a size K (6.5 mm) hook.

**Finished Size**

When placed flat, this piece measures 32 by 39 inches.

**Yardage**

Each of the three colors needs one skein. Each skein included 220 yards of yarn. Most of the cream hue was utilized, as well as 170 yards of grey and pink.

**Abbreviations for Stitches**

- ch-chain
- ch space stands for chain space.
- single crochet sc
- extended single crochet - esc
- beginning chain -beg ch

**Explanations for Stitches**

Put your hook into another st and draw up the loop, yarn over & draw through 1 loop, yarn over & pull through the other two loops on hook: 1 esc done

**Gauge**

5 esc stitches equal 5 inches

Ch 60, using the cream-colored yarn. To expand the breadth of your blanket, ch any even number.

Row 1: 1 sc in second ch from hook & each ch across (work this row tight). -59 sc

Row 2: Chain 3 (counts as an extended single crochet+ ch 1) skip next st, extended single crochet in next, *(chain 1, skip next st, extended single crochet in next), rep from * to end.

Row 3: Chain 3 (counts as an extended single crochet+ ch 1), sk the next st, extended single crochet in next, *(ch 1, skip next st, extended single crochet in next), rep from * to end.

**Note:** It can be found that putting your final st into the starting ch 1 created a straighter edge than working into the starting ch-2 at the finish of Row 3.

Row 4: Chain 3 (tallies as esc+ chain 1), sk the next st, 1 extended single crochet in next ch-space, *(chain 1, skip the next st, 1 esc in next chain-space), rep from * to last 2 sts (esc + beg ch), ch 1, skip next esc, 1 esc on top of starting ch-2, connect pink color yarn, fasten off cream color yarn.

**Note:** Rows 3 and 4 will be alternated with color changes in between.

Row 5: In color pink, repeat Row 3, joining color grey at the last of a row, & fasten off the pink. Turn around.

Row 6: In color grey, repeat Row 4, joining the color cream at the last of the row & fastening off the grey. Turn around.

Row 7: In color cream, repeat Row 3, joining color pink at the last of the row and fastening off the cream. Turn around.

Row 8: In color pink, repeat Row 4, joining color cream at the last of the row, & fasten off the pink. Turn around.

Row 9-23: In color cream, alternate Rows 3 and 4, joining color pink at the last of Row 23, & fastening off the color cream. Turn around.

**Notes:**

1. You may change the length of the blanket by crocheting more or less rows here, but be sure you keep track of the amount of rows for the next two panels.

2. From the top of a pink row, the cream panel measured roughly 9 1/2 inches.

Rows 24–38: Work in color pink for the following 15 rows, joining color grey at the completion of Row 38, then fasten off the pink. Turn around.

Row 55: In color cream, repeat Row 3, connect grey at the last of a row, & fasten off the color cream. Turn around.

Row 56: In color grey, repeat Row 4, connect pink at the last of the row, and fasten off color grey. Turn around.

Row 57: In color pink, repeat Row 3, joining cream at the last of the row and fastening off the pink. Turn around.

Rows 58-60: In color cream, repeat Rows 4, 3, and 4. Invert the situation.

Row 61: chain 2 (count as a hdc), 1 of hdc in each chain & st across to finish, fasten off.—-60 hdc

Note: Because the hdc makes the same size as the first colourful panel, the final row is an hdc row rather than a single crochet row from the first row.

**Finishing**

Weave in all the remaining tails using the smaller hook. To prevent your tails from displaying through the gaps, weave through the top half of your esc sts.

Row 39-53: For the following 15 rows, repeat Rows 3 & 4 in color grey, joining color pink at the bottom of Row 53, then fasten off the color grey. Turn around.

Row 54: In color pink, repeat Row 4, joining color cream at the bottom of the row and fastening off the color pink. Turn around.

## 4.3 Crochet Hat Pattern

Skill: Beginners, Time: 90 minutes

This crochet hat design for beginners is really simple, whether you simply need a fast project or new to crocheting. This basic unisex beanie design may be made by anybody who can crochet a rectangle.

To create a great tapered form, crocheting a hat typically requires a fair bit of counting when increasing or decreasing. This isn't the case. You'll use the most elementary crochet stitches to produce a gorgeously traditional ribbed beanie with this novel method. (Preemie through adult sizes)

**Supplies:**

- Wool-Ease Tonal Lion Brands – 2 skeins (Weight: 5 per bulky – 124 yards, 4 oz.) Smoke (635-149) & Slate Blue are the colors seen (635-107)
- Needle for tapestry
- Crochet hook, size L (8 millimeters)
- Safety pins or stitch markers
- Small piece of cardboard/ pom pom maker or fur pom pom

**Dimensions**:

S: Young adolescent (circumference of about 18" unstretched)

M: The majority of women and men (unstretched circumference: approx. 20")

L: Heads with a larger circumference (about 22" unstretched circumference)

## Gauge:

4" = 10 stitches

4" = little over 4 rows

## Glossary and Abbreviations (US Terms):

- ch (chain)
- dcblo - Double crochet via the back loop
- tch stands for "turning chain."
- sk – (skip)
- st - (stitch)
- RS stands for right side.
- WS stands for Wrong side
- rep – (repeat)

## Notes on the Overall Pattern:

The pattern has been written in size S, with M & L in brackets. S (M/L)

## Notes:

- A hat is crocheted in rows back and forth. These rows will produce the beanie's vertical ribs.
- The chain (Ch) 3 at the start of each row is not counted as a stitch.
- To make this crochet hat design fit a toddler, start with less stitches & work fewer total stitches.

- After Row 1, doubled crochet stitches are only crocheted beneath the back loop of the preceding row's thread. Regardless of whatever side of the crochet is facing you, this is the loop farthest distant from you.

Ch 37 foundation row.

Row 1: 1 dc in the fourth ch from hook & each chain (ch) to end of row; turn (34)

Row 2: Dcblo (double crochet through the back loop only) in each dc to the end of the row; turn (34)

Row 2 should be repeated 16 (18, 20) the most times for a maximum of 18 (20, 22) rows.

Leaving a 24 inches tail, fasten off.

The size of the rectangle should be approximate:

18" x 14.5" (S)

20" x 14.5" (M)

22" x 14.5" (L)

**Seaming Rectangle**

**Notes:**

To calculate your fabric's RS and WS, do the following: Whenever the WS is facing, the tail of the last row must be on the left bottom if you're right-handed. If you're left-handed, the top left corner of your last row should have the WS facing you.

The seam is worked just via the chain stitches & the loop of each dc st closest to the seam to hide the junction.

With the WS facing up, lay the rectangle horizontally. If desired, use safety pins or stitch markers to pin the seam.

Tapestry needle having tail from fastening off threaded from both the top of the dc stitch, work into the top of the matching chain. Then, starting at the end of the following chain, work into the end of the adjacent dc. Carry on in this manner from the top of 1 dc to a top of 1 chain, then from the end of one chain to the bottom of 1 dc. Rep till the seam is finished.

Enter needle into crochet cloth to make a loop of yarn, now insert the needle into loop of yarn & pull tight to tie a basic sewing knot. This will avoid the puckering of the seam in the following step. Trim the yarn but do not cut it.

**Top Closing**

Whipstitch across the top of the hat using tapestry needle & strand of yarn leftover from the last seam, working 1 whip stitch through each row. Tighten the circles as much as possible, then stitch up any residual openings in the hat's top using a tapestry needle.

**Adding a Pom Pom**

Use a huge pom-pom machine or a 2.5" piece of cardboard to create a pom-pom. A gradual pom-pom technique may be found here.

How to create the pom-pom for a beanie in crochet or knit. The color "slate blue" is Lion Brands Wool-Ease Tonal yarn.

Sew pom pom fur or yarn to the hat using the tail left over from the seam.

Finish by tying off any loose ends and weaving them in.

Put the new crochet hat upon your head and start creating more for your friends and family.

## 4.4 Pattern for Crochet Slipper Sock

**Supplies:**

Made Easy Yarn Lion Brands Color, 54 to 157 yards or 1.52 to 4.44 Oz

Crochet Hook, Size K, 6.5 mm

Needle for yarn

A pair of scissors

**Abbreviations and Stitches**

- CH stands for the chain.
- SC stands for Single Crochet.
- DC stands for Double Crochet.
- SLST stands for Slip Stitch.
- ST(s) stands for Stitch (es)
- MC stands Magic Circle

**Size & Gauge**

2 inches = 3 Rows x 6 DC

By adding additional rows to the heel portion or toe, the length of a crochet slipper sock may be easily altered.

**Notes:**

- It's written in American terms.
- Your turning chain (chain 2) doesn't really count as the stitch.
- This design is designed for a toddler, with a kid and tiny women's size in brackets. When the patterns are done in the same way for all sizes, notes are provided.

Rows 1 & 2 are done in the same way regardless of size.

Toe Row 1: SLST to first DC, work 12 Double Crochet (DC) into a Magic Circle. (12)

Toe Row 2: Chain (CH2), *DC (direct crochet) into the next 03 STs, 02DC into the next ST* 3 times more. To the first DC, SLST. (Fifteenth)

Skip row 3 & continue on row 4 for the Toddler Size.

Toe Row 3: Chain (CH2), *DC into the next 4 Stitch (STs), 02DC into the next stitch* 3 times more. To the first DC, SLST. (18)

CH2, DC into following 15 (18, 18) Stitches (STs) on Toe Row 3(4, 4). To the first DC, SLST. (15, 17, 18, 19)

Row 3 should be repeated four times for the toddler size.

Rep row 4 a whole of the 5 times for the kid-size.

Rep row 4 a maximum of 7 times for the small women's size.

The toe section has been completed.

## Heel of Slipper

You must have 6 rows completed for the size of toddler, 8 rows completed for the kid-size, and 10 rows completed for the small women's size at this point.

Heel Row 1: Chain 2, Dc into the next 12(15, 14) Stitches. (12, 15, 14)

Heel Row 2: Chain 2, turn, Dc into the next 12(15, 14) Stitches. (12, 15, 14)

Rep Heel Row 2 twice more for toddler size.

Rep Heel Row 2 three times for the kid-size.

Repeat Heel Row 2 four times for the small women's size.

The heel part is now complete.

## Cuff for Slippers

We'll work 2 single crocheted into the side of every heel row for the slipper cuff, then single crocheted into the unworked stitch of Heel Row 1. Then, on the opposite side of the rows of heels, knit 2 single crochet.

Row 1 of the cuff: CH1, 2 SC in each of the following 3(4, 5) rows. Incorporate Single crochet (sc) into the following 3(3, 4) Stitches. In the following 3(4, 5) rows, work 2 single crochet (sc) into the side. To the first SC, SLST. (15, 19, 24)

Row 1 of the cuff is finished.

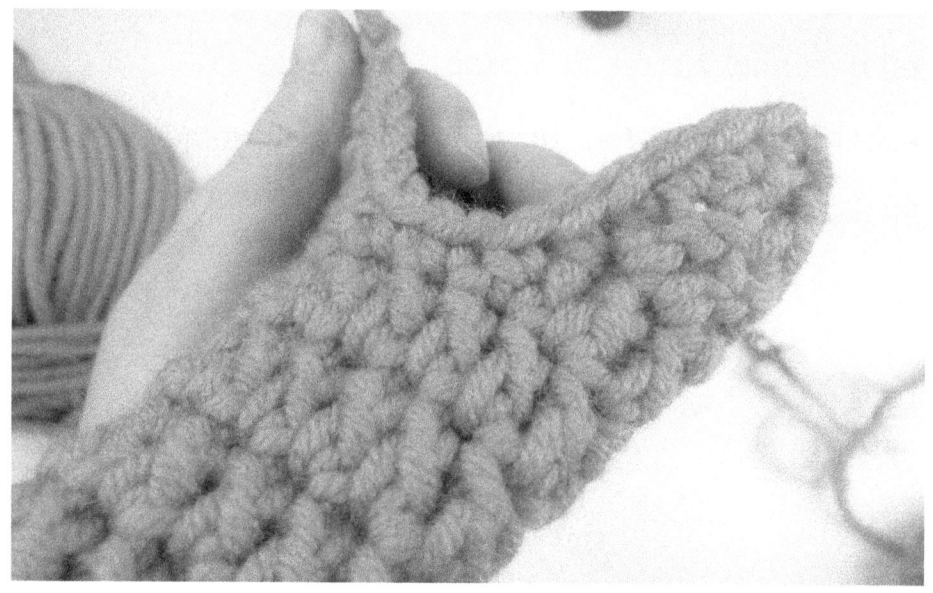

Cuff Row 2-3: CH2, DC on next 15 (19 to 24) Stitches. To the first DC, SLST.

Fasten off here for the toddler & kid sizes, leaving long yarn ends to stitch up the heel.

Cuff Row 4 (For Size, Small Women): CH2, Double Crochet (DC) into the next 24 Stitches. To the first DC, SLST. Finish with a longer yarn end to stitch up the heel.

Thread the yarn end onto a needle and weave it through the cuff row to the open heel to finish the crochet slipper socks. Sew up the heel using an invisible stitch or a whip stitch.

## 4.5 Market Bag Pattern

This basic crochet design creates trendy crochet market bags with plaid design or gingham using basic colorwork. This is a simple stash buster design that takes just one skein within each color. For a final touch, attach a ranch house rope handle or start crochet one's own.

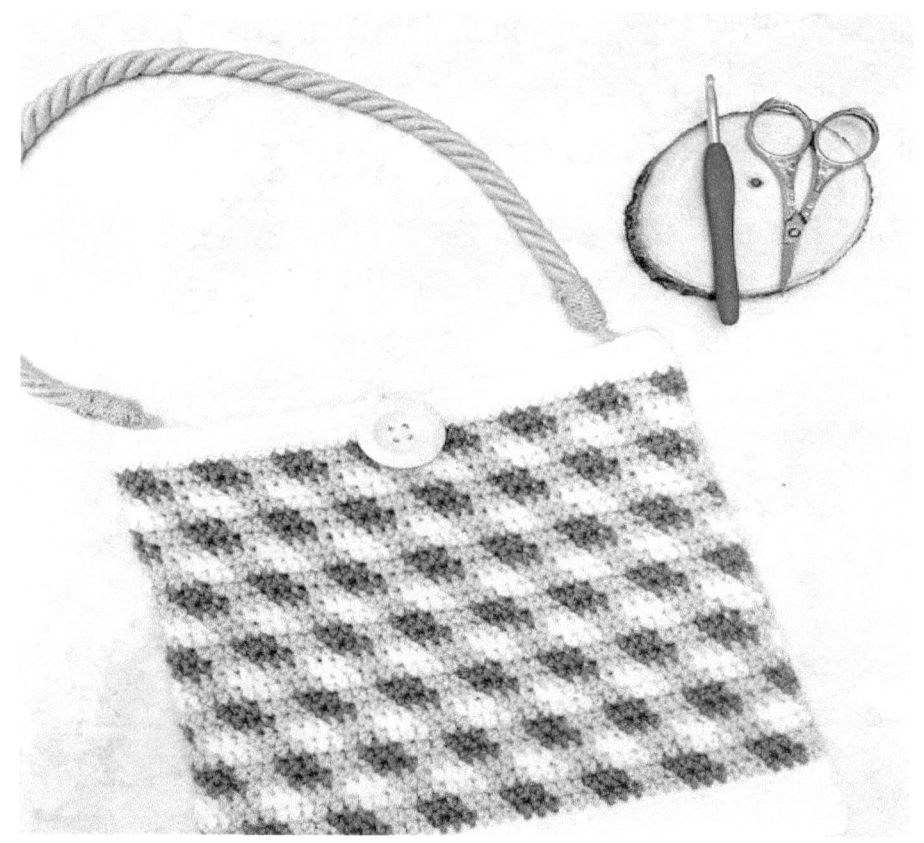

## Supplies:

- Three colors of worsted weight yarn each color requires less than 170 yards. You can use Lion Brand Vanna's Choice & Loops & Threads Impeccable together.
- Crochet hook, H/5.0 mm
- Yarn Needle
- Scissors
- Handbag straps (one can easily get it from amazon)
- Button (1 1/2") (optional)

## Abbreviations (in American terms):

- YO stands for yarn over.
- Ch stands for chain.

- Sl st stands for slip stitch.
- SC stands for single crochet.
- HDC stands for half double crochet.

**Gauge**

6-row x 9 sts = 2" squares In HDC,

**Finished Dimensions:**

10.5" in width

12" in length (without the strap).

**Notes on the Pattern**

The chain stitch at the start of each round does not qualify as a stitch.

An sl st is used to attach the ending of each round to the start stitch of the round.

Color A is white, Color B is light green, and Color C is dark green. The color green

We suggest carrying the yarn for color changes to reduce the number of endings to weave into it at the finish.

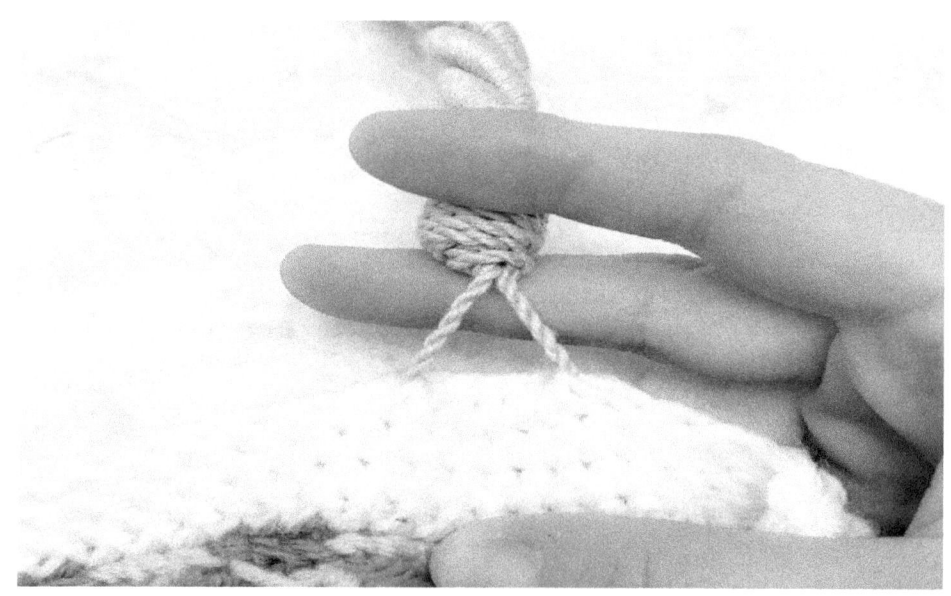

Begin with Color A.

Chain 44

Round 1: SC in the second chain (ch) from hook, Single Crochet (SC) in 41, 2 SC in the final chain (front side of ch). SC in 42, 2 Single Crochet (SC) in the final stitch on the rear (backside of chain) (this would be the 1st stitch you worked on the front). With an sl st, join the first single crochet (SC) of the round (88)

Round 2: (Chain) ch 1, *SC (single crochet) in 43, 2 SC (single crochet) in the next stitch, repeat from *, link with an sl st to the first SC (single crochet) of the round (90)

Rounds 3–10: Chain 1, SC all around, sl st to first SC (90)

Rounds 11-12 (Begin with Color B): (Chain) ch 1, *HDC into 3 stitches with Colors B, HDC in next 03 stitches with Color C, rep from * 14 times more. With an sl st, join to the 1st HDC of the round (90).

Rounds 13-14: ch 1, **HDC in first 3 stitches with Colors A, HDC into next 3 stitches with Colors B, rep from * 14 times more. With an sl st, join to the 1st HDC of the round (90).

Rounds 11-12 are repeated in Rounds 15-16.

Rounds 13-14 are repeated in Rounds 17-18.

Rounds 11-12 are repeated in rounds 19-20.

Rounds 13-14 are repeated in rounds 21-22.

Rounds 11-12 are repeated in rounds 23-24.

Repeat Rounds 13-14 in Rounds 25-26.

Rounds 11-12 are repeated in rounds 27-28.

Rounds 13-14 are repeated in Rounds 29-30.

Rounds 31-32 are the same as Rounds 11-12.

Rounds 13-14 are repeated in rounds 33-34.

Rounds 11-12 are repeated in rounds 35-36.

Rounds 37-39 (A Color): (Chain) ch 1, SC all around, sl st to first SC (90)

Round 40: (Chain) ch 1, SC in 20, Single crochet over handle loops for next 08 stitches, Single crochet in 37, Single crochet over handles loop for next 08 stitches, Single Crochet in 17, connect to first single crochet of the rounds with an sl st. Tight

Chain 10, skip 2 stitches & connect with an sl st to make a button loop.

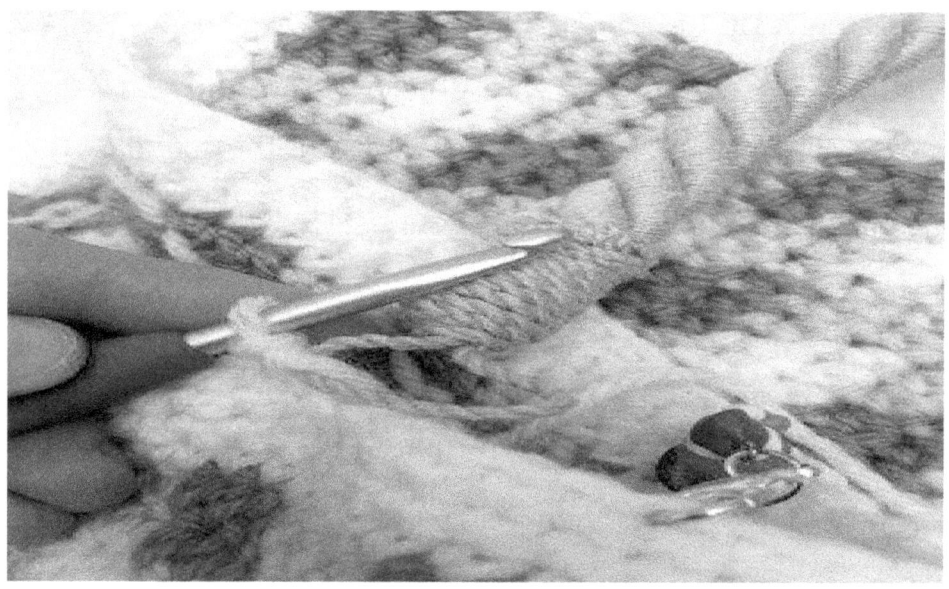

Note that the button loop is an optional feature. Finish the round of single crochet as normal if you don't want a button closing. Weave in all ends, Tie off yarn, and, if desired, attach a button.

# Chapter 5: Wearing the Crochet

Antique doilies and old sweaters may come to mind when you think about crochet. Crochet tops, on the other hand, have made a comeback in a big manner. Crochet shirts come in a variety of styles, from large blouses to small crop tops, and are an essential part of any summer wardrobe. Learn which undergarments to wear along with crochet, what bottoms to match it with, as well as how to accessorize it flawlessly if you're adopting the trend.

## 5.1 Selecting Undergarments

1. Wear a tank top with no sleeves beneath. It might be difficult to choose a crochet top since they might look to be excessively exposed. Underneath your crochet top, a nude camisole is a right answer. It would not blend in or detract from the crochet design, which is the highlight of your ensemble if you choose a nude hue. You're also completely covered, so there's no need to be concerned about overexposure or seeming indecent.

2. Wear a bandeau or bralette beneath. You may choose not to cover yourself fully beneath your crochet top if you're feeling brave. Try putting it over a bandeau or a bralette instead. Bralettes are comparable to bras, however, they don't have underwire and don't seem as much like underwear as a standard bra. [2] Bandeaus are some kind of tube top that covers your chest with a strip of fabric. You could keep

your tummy visible in your crochet shirt while yet cover up your chest by wearing any of them beneath it.

Bralettes with all types of lovely details are available, & both bralettes & bandeaus are available in a number of colors. From under your crochet top, you may pick a lovely item to give interest to your ensemble.

3. Wear something bright beneath. You don't have to limit yourself to neutral tanks & underwear. In fact, a splash of color may be added to your look by wearing a royal blue tank top, a pink bra, or a bright scarlet bandeau beneath a crochet top. Make the rest of the outfit simple and allow the bright undergarment to draw attention to the top's design.

Try matching plain black shorts with such a black crochet shirt, but add a bright red camisole beneath for a splash of color.

By layering a neon color bandeau beneath jeans & a white crochet top, you may make the outfit more unique.

## 5.2 How to Wear a Crochet Top?

1. Wear your crochet shirt with a pair of jeans. Pair your crochet shirt with such a pair of jeans or shorts to keep the rest of your outfit casual. For a more informal, flower kid look, go for a tattered pair. Choose sleek and darker denim to spice up your look a little more. Jeans are a no-brainer since they work with every crochet top, regardless of style or color.

Wear a flowy, boho crochet top with holes and rips in your faded denim. This is a light and airy summer style. Wear a much more structured crochet shirt with a dark wash, cut jeans for a more formal look.

2. Use colourful, interesting designs in your crochet. With this suggestion, you may really embrace the hippy mood. Pair a solid-colored crocheted top with a vivid and eye-catching design on shorts, skirts, or trousers. Combining crochet with such a pattern is a much more daring option, and your ensemble will undoubtedly stand out.

Wear a flowery or paisley-patterned pair of shorts with a white crochet blouse. Wear a neutral-colored crochet blouse with a classic tie-dyed skirt.

3. Wear a maxi skirt for a bohemian style. It's really about balance if it comes to putting together a nice look. If you're wearing a little, sultry crochet blouse, balance out your look with a floor-length maxi skirt. The ideal bohemian garment is a lovely flowing maxi skirt. You may create a wonderful silhouette & strike the ideal mix between modest & risqué by matching it with a much form-fitting & exposing crochet top.

 A miniskirt with a small crochet crop top may reveal more flesh than you like, while billowy skirts with a loose, floating crochet top may not produce the most complimentary silhouette.

Wear a high-waisted maxi with a cropped crochet shirt. You'll get a slim silhouette and show a little flesh without going overboard.

4. Pair it with a pair of dressy pants. Crochet may be worn without making you appear like you're going to a music festival or the beach. You may surely dress up your crochet shirt and wear it in a much more professional situation. It's all about equilibrium once again. Wear a more sophisticated pair of slacks or pencil skirt with your more informal crochet top. Combine an unstructured crocheted top with fitted pants to create a striking contrast.

It's ideal to combine your crochet top with a full-coverage tank top if you're wearing it to work.

Wear a tailored jacket over your crochet top to make it appear more professional.

5. Wear a monotone ensemble with your crochet shirt. Crochet is a great way to add interest to an outfit. Try layering a crochet shirt over a monochromatic outfit to add some interest. If you have a favorite black dress, experiment with adding a crochet layer to it. Try a multicolored crochet shirt over white slacks & a white tank top. You have a plethora of choices. In a monochromatic ensemble, a crochet shirt might be the ideal standout item.

## 5.3 Crochet Top Accessorizing

1. Wear some bright earrings. When it comes to crochet tops, the design usually has a lot going on. Chunky necklaces will draw attention away from the crochet, while small necklaces will blend in. Earring is one of the greatest ways to match it with jewelry. Pair exquisite, intricate crochet with much more delicate earrings, and bulky crochet tops with more simple earrings.

Rather of distracting from or contrasting with the crochet design, the earrings should complement it.

Wear a basic cream crochet shirt with flamboyant feather earrings, for example. Consider wearing something eye-catching, bright-colored earrings if your ensemble is monochromatic or more neutral.

2. Don a slouchy cardigan. A crochet shirt may not even be warm enough on colder days. Thankfully, these shirts look well with loose cardigans! Crochet shirts, especially those that are tighter or skimpier, look great with loose-fitting, easy sweaters. Find a cardigan that has the same weight & texture as the top and drape it loosely over your shoulders.

Wear a lightweight, flowy cardigan with a flowing crochet top. Cardigans that are thin yet large look great with crochet shirts.

3. Add some bangles to your ensemble. Nothing goes better with such a crocheted top than a wonderful bangle or

collection of bangles whenever it comes to bracelets. Because a crochet top's design is more organic & a solid, free-flowing, geometric bracelet contrasts wonderfully. Choose the simpler patterns; you won't need to add anything to these tops.

4. Match your crochet top with a handbag or bag. Instead of opting for an extremely structured, hefty handbag, go for a lighter, unstructured version. Fringed or floral-print bags will go well with the boho aesthetic. Lightweight cross-body bags can store all of your belongings while being casual and unobtrusive.

# Chapter 6: Crochet Gifts & Home Decor

Crocheting is increasingly becoming a popular pastime among many people. Even if you're new to knitting, there are a plethora of delightfully simple designs to choose from. In actuality, there are a few items that you may start crocheting right now and complete before the ending of the day. To share with you, I've gathered 30 of my favorite beginning crochet designs. These items would also make great presents, so if you're in a hurry and need a present, grab your crochet hooks & get started.

We have to confess that we like getting homemade presents, and we are ready to wager that we are not alone. One can be assured that there is a pattern that will help you choose a present for anybody. Most of them take an hour or less to complete, making them fast presents that are also simple to crochet. This crochet for the beginner's book also includes a lot of fantastic gift ideas. They're also simple patterns and tasks that may usually be completed in an hour or less.

Patterns for beginners are essential while learning how to crochet. They're simple to read, and you'll be able to practice and master fundamental stitches before going on to more difficult designs. Of obviously, you would like to learn much more than single crochet, and therefore this collection includes designs that employ a variety of stitches — they're all simple to learn, but you won't be trapped repeating the same stitch in each one. They're also ideal for people who have learned crochet and are looking for quick and simple present ideas.

The following are some items that can be crocheted in less than an hour and given as gifts or used to decorate one's house. It's crucial to note that these are merely names; instructions for making them may be found in the chapter of the project.

- Beautiful Crochet Gloves
- Delicate Shoes for Toddlers
- Crochet Cardigan
- Crochet Hexagon Sweater
- Pineapple Crochet Hat
- Crochet Potholder
- Crochet Mitten
- Crochet Hand Bags
- Crochet Socks & Slippers
- Crochet Curtains, Rags & Baskets for Home Décor
- Crochet Wall Hangings
- Crochet Ornaments

You can easily give all these items as gifts to your loved ones and if you have gone through this book you will be able to do it on your own within no time. So wait no more time and start crocheting right now.

# Conclusion

This book is appropriate for all crocheters, including those with little prior experience and those with very advanced capabilities. If you've never used a crochet hook earlier but would like to learn, the book will walk you through all of the fundamental stitches so you can produce stunning tiny and big objects. If you also know well how to crochet, there is a tremendous choice of unusual and lovely designs to try out at a reasonable price.

Crochet takes you through the fundamental stitches and methods, presenting them clearly & simply with step-by-step images and explaining the abbreviations and symbols along the way. Beginners may work their way through the book's first portions thorough and easy-to-follow methods section, pausing along with the attempt to stimulate out such a tiny item to practice the stitch they've just learned. This book may also be used by more experienced crocheters to review stitches they already know. From basic chains stitch bracelets to a beautiful intarsia cushion, the little crafts are diverse. Once you've mastered all of the crochet stitches, go on to the crafts section and start crocheting things like a classic granny blanket for a newborn, a little sock for a toddler, & small girl's market bag.

There's something for everyone with over 80 projects to pick from, including blankets and pillows, hats and scarves, gloves, socks, and slippers, household goods, clothing and bags, and a variety of lovely toys to create. Crochet allows you to create one-of-a-kind crocheted items for your home, yourself, and your family & friends.

**Book Two**

# CROCHET

The Quick Easy Way To Learn Crocheting To Find Out The Basic Techniques and Create Fun and Easy Patterns For All The Family.

# Introduction

The actual roots of crochet are veiled in a shroud of mystery. Other needlecrafts, such as weaving, embroidery, and cross-stitch, may be traced back in time using pictorial data, historical records, and written documents, but crochet falls short in these contexts.

Crochet is derived from the French word 'crochet,' which means 'hook.' This linguistic insight may imply that the French performed a vital role in its invention, but there is no evidence to support this claim. Instead, historians and crochet experts have assembled a list of possible explanations, each giving a different explanation about how this technique came into existence.

Crochet has also been discovered among the ancestors of Guiana Indians. Crochet, according to Lis Paludan, originated in Asia and spread westward to Spain, then eastward to Tibet through Arab trade routes. She also believes that crochet originated in South America and was used to create adornments for puberty rites. Three-dimensional dolls were discovered in China as early models of crochet.

Although no one knows for sure where crochet originated, it is now one of the most common yarn crafts, with devotees from all over the world. Crochet may be used to make clothing, furniture, home décor, gifts, jewelry, and fiber art.

You will find this book very interesting, covering all the topics related to the crochet technique ranging from introduction to several techniques and products. In this book, you will find a lot of techniques to start crocheting. It ranges from simpler to complex ones. To have a bird's eye view read the following points, but you will have to go through the book for a complete understanding.

- Introduction to Crochet
- Tools and requirements
- Types of Crochet
- Techniques of using crochet.
- Crochet projects
- Crochet products

# Chapter: 1 Introduction to Crochet

The roots of crochet are a point of contention. Many scholars say crochet originated in 16th century Europe and was known as chain lace or crochet lace. Crochet, also known as nun's lace or nun's job, may have been around the 15th century. Today's thread doilies look a lot like nun's lace, but they're not as complex.

There are three possible historical hypotheses about the origin of crochet. The first possibility is that crochet may have started in Arabia and spread eastward to Tibet, westward to Spain, and finally to other Mediterranean countries through Arab trade routes. Second, it may have started in South America, where a native group is believed to have crocheted designs for puberty rituals. Third, the roots may have been in

China, where dolls were considered to be crocheted on a daily basis.

It is necessary to keep in mind that these are all hypotheses. Finally, there is no solid proof that crochet started in either of these locations or at either of these times periods. When we move down to the 18th century, though, the past gets a bit clearer.

Crochet is thought to have originated from a Chinese needlework technique known as 'tambourine,' which is identical to modern-day crochet. Tambourine, unlike crochet, was made on silk using fine yarn and a gripped needle. When this needlecraft made its way to Europe, it was discovered that threaded chains could indeed hold together without backing yarn, and hence crochet was born!

This groundbreaking realization came just in time, as Ireland was hit by the devastating potato famine in the 1840s, plunging the nation into poverty. Many Irish families depended on potato crops for food, but the majority of them were afflicted with potato blight, necessitating the search for a new source of income.

Mademoiselle Riego, better remembered for her crochet designs, brought this newfound art to the citizens of Ireland, providing the world with a whole new exchange. Crochet seemed to meet any of the criteria. Not only were the supplies readily available, but the project could also be completed in the daytime and by candlelight, regardless of the season!

Crochet gave Irish employees a chance to learn a new talent, raise money, and, most importantly, feed their families. Crochet quickly traveled across the globe as Irish people started to flee to the United Kingdom and America.

Crochet has continued to grow to this day, dividing into several various ways. 'Granny squares' are a throwback to World War II, where helpless grandmothers will save any bit of fabric in the hopes of crocheting it into bigger bits, or 'granny squares,' as we now call them.

# Chapter: 2 Tools and Requirements

Basic Crochet Materials for Beginners are listed below.

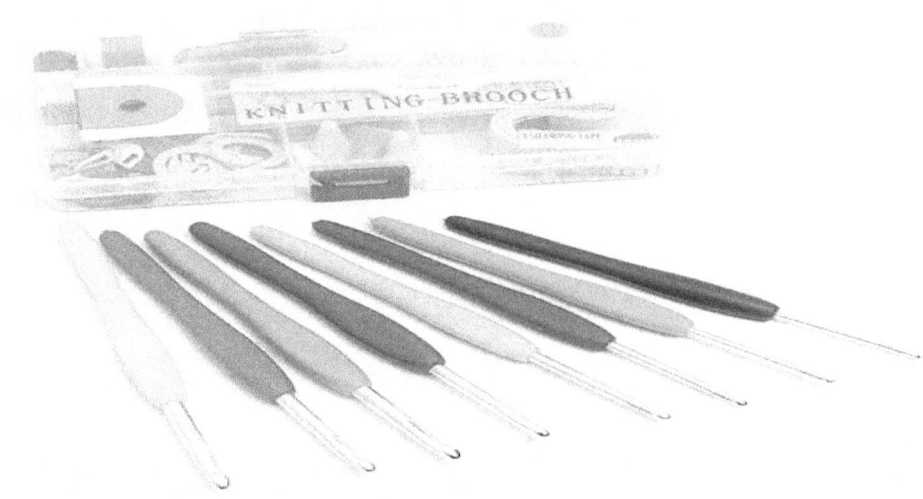

## 1. Crochet hook

Hooks come in a variety of shapes and sizes, as well as a variety of materials. Assess which hook would be more useful for you.

## 2. Yarn

Purchasing yarn is a fun experience that will lift your spirits and get you thinking about upcoming activities. Yarns are manufactured from a variety of fabrics, so do some analysis and see which one would be better for your project.

## 3.Darning needle

A darning needle for crocheting, unlike a sewing needle, has a large eye for fabric or fabric inserting. You will insert the thread even more easily than using a sewing needle. It is used to join the ends of the product in crochet.

## 4.Scissors

Scissors are the third item on the list. Scissors are an essential crochet tool that can never be left at home! Sewing scissors, including wool and crochet pins, come in a

variety of styles and purposes.

## 5.Hook organizer

You can create this useful hook organizer with cloth, yarn, and a needle! To keep all of your crochet hooks organized.

## 6.Stitch Markers

Stitch markers are adorable clips that can be used to indicate where your pattern begins and ends. If you are operating on a circular pattern, this is especially helpful.

Stitch markers are not absolutely required when you are first starting out, and not every pattern needs them. However, you will hope you had a package of stitch markers at any stage during your crochet adventure.

Stitch markers may be used in a variety of ways, including:

- If you are crocheting a big project, stitch markers will help you maintain track of the rows, so you don't lose track.
- They are used to keep a record of the first stitch of a round while crocheting in the round. This is advantageous when making amigurumi.
- Stitch markers come in handy while making a dress, particularly for labeling armholes and holding panels together when stitching.

Plus, there is a slew of other options that you will discover!

## 7. Measurement tape

Crocheting is a very flexible craft. Tape measures are commonly used as a sewing tool, but they are also an important crochet tool for precision, particularly if you are following a template.

## 8. Stitch Patterns

Crochet Patterns are used as a reference where accuracy is desired.

## 9. Crochet Book

It includes a variety of templates, details, and instructions for making lovely crochet

designs.

## 10. Row Counter

Column counters come in a variety of shapes and sizes, and this one is referred to as a mechanical row counter. It contains the details of your crocheting projects and saves you a lot of time!

## 11. Crochet Materials Organizer

This crochet tool organizer might be useful to you. We recommend that you make yours the same size so that you can get it in. Tape steps, thread, the hook organizer, and other items are held in organizers. This should be a perfect place to keep all of your crocheting supplies.

## 12. Aluminum & Plastic

Aluminum and acrylic hooks are inexpensive and come in a variety of sizes. Both are fantastic! And are regarded as important crochet tools.

# Chapter: 3 Types of Crochet

## 1. Crochet type one (amigurumi style)

It is a Japanese crochet artistic expression that relates to the creation of tiny soft toys or animals out of crocheted yarn. It is amigurumi whenever you see a little toy of children.

Crochet products utilizing the amigurumi technique are the following.

- Toys for kids
- Fan items
- Pillows and large-sized house goods

## 2. Crochet type two (Bavarian)

It is an antique crochet stitch that is traditionally used to make granny squares in rounds. It produces a dense fabric with a softer texture than granny squares which makes for more subtle color adjustments. Each column is divided into two sections. Bavarian crochet resembles a rather fancy version of granny squares.

Crochet Products utilizing the Bavarian technique are the following.

- Blankets are one of the things you can create with Bavarian Crochet.
- Shawls are a popular option.

## 3. Crochet type three (Bruges)

This technique is used to produce Bruges lace, which consists of creating crochet "ribbons" that are then knitted together to shape elaborate lace designs. Most grandmothers have several Bruges-style crochet pieces tucked away in drawers, covered in acid-free paper.

Products.

- Intricate shawls
- Fabric embellishments
- Tablecloths

## 4. Crochet type four (Bullion)

It is a unique crochet stitch that is made by wrapping several yarn wraps covering a lengthy hook to create a prominent and unusual 'roll' stitch. This crochet pattern is typically used for patterns rather than projects that include yarn. It produces an item with a dense, standardized circular motif.

Products obtained utilizing this technique are the following.

- Objects that are stiff, such as placemats, are important products of this technique.
- Decoration motifs

## 5. Crochet type five (Broomstick)
This antique crochet stitch, also known as jiffy lace, is created using a conventional crochet hook, except the crocheting is done around some lengthy object, such as a long stick. The

produced lace is a great crochet talent to master because it produces a stunning and one-of-a-kind finished product.

Products obtained utilizing this technique are the following.

- Delicate shawls may be made using this crochet technique.
- Decorative blankets

## 6. Crochet type six (Aran)

Ribbed or cabled crochet is what this term refers to. It is a textured crochet pattern of interlocking cables that can be used to create beanies, sweaters, and scarves.

Crochet projects utilizing this technique are the following.

- blankets
- Coats
- Scarves
- Jackets

## 7.Crochet type seven(clothesline)

Common crochet stitches are employed over a dense loop to create round mats and bins that keep their form. This is a trial method that can be followed back to Nepalese and African craftspeople.

Crochet Projects to create with the Clothesline hook are the following.

- Baskets

- Mats
- Wall hangings with structural elements

## 8. Crochet type eight (Bosnian)

Bosnian crochet uses just the crochet slip stitch, which is worked in separate sections of a stitch from the previous row, to create a dense, knit-like cloth. Bosnian crochet hooks are available for purchase, but standard crochet hooks can also be used. Shepherd's knitting is another name for it. It also resembles knitting in appearance. It is not a really fashionable look right now, and if you see it, you will probably assume it is knitted.

Crochet projects utilizing this technique are the following.

- Scarves
- Beanies
- Smaller objects, since it takes a long time.

## 9. Crochet type nine (Clones Lace)

This crochet design is closely related to Irish lace crochet and was developed as an alternative to needlepoint lace since it was much faster and simpler to make. The Clone knot is a crochet skill that belongs to the clone's crochet ability collection. Clone's lace is a very functional crochet pattern that was used during wars for utilitarian purposes.

Products obtained utilizing the clone lace technique are the following.

- Openwork scarves are a great way to use the clone's lace style of crochet.
- Skirts and tops for a delicate appearance

## 10.Crochet type ten (Tunisian)

Tunisian crochet is identical to spinning in that you have several live loops at every given moment, and you work the loops on and off your hook, much like knitting. Tunisian crochet is done on a lengthy hook with a blocker at the end or a hook with a string attached.

**Tunisian crochet projects**

- Objects that seem to be knitted

- Blankets are one of the most common items seen in a home.
- Scarves

## 11. Crochet type eleven (Filet)

Chains and double crochet are used to make this crochet pattern. It is a grid-like design of squares that are either filled or not filled, with negative space used to generate pictures inside the object. Filet crochet is unusual in that it allows you to use both entire and empty squares of fabric to embed photos.

**Crochet projects** that use the fillet method are the following.

- Blankets for children
- Coats, kimonos, and other outerwear
- Bag
- Pillow covers.

## 12. Crochet type twelve (Hairpin)

This is identical to broomstick crochet, but the crochet piece is kept taut between two thin metal poles instead of a broomstick. This method was named for the usage of real metal hairpins at the time it was created. This technique produces a fabric that is really one-of-a-kind.

## 13. Crochet type thirteen(finger)

Finger crochet is identical to finger knitting, but it does not include the use of a needle. It is basically a kind of Crochet stitched hand cloth weaving. When you first start out, finger crochet is a lot of fun, but since the finished tension is too loose, you will want to move to a hook to create more versatile projects easily.

**Crochet Projects** to create with your finger technique are the following.

- Bags made from string.
- Scarves that are not too fancy

## 14. Crochet type fourteen (Microns)

This is a contemporary crochet design that uses very fine yarn and crochet hooks. This is a really delicate job, and it's possibly better left to crocheters who are more careful.

Crochet projects with microns technique are the following.

- Small-sized items
- Additions to the design
- Symbols

## 15. Crochet type fifteen (freeform)

This crochet style is made without the use of a template or a set of instructions. Crochet in this style is really natural and decorative. Note that if you are a control freak, this style might not be for you.

Crochet projects obtained by the freeform technique are the following.

- Items of art
- One-time offing clothes

## 16. Crochet type sixteen (Pineapple)

It is like a stitch and form pattern than a method. Pinafores may be used to create doilies, scarves, and even clothing in crochet. Once you have learned to recognize a crochet pineapple, you will see them all over the place. In the 1970s, this stitch became common.

Crochet Projects create by this technique are the following.

- Formal wear
- tops
- dress
- Shawls are a common accessory.
- Tissues

## 17. Crochet type seventeen (symbol)

This is also described as chart crochet, and it is a common stitch pattern in Japanese stitch books. It is a really useful ability to master, and you can use any symbol crochet book in any language to complete the tasks simply by following the map.

Note: Learning to Crochet from symbol patterns can transform your life.

Crochet symbols may be used to create a variety of products.

- Difficult-to-understand trends.
- Aesthetics with a lot of detail
- Variations in different languages

## 18. Crochet type eighteen (overlay)

A raised pattern is created by starting with a base of crochet and then adding stitches on top of it. This opens up a world of possibility for stunning colorwork.

Crochet overlays may be used to render a variety of different items.

- Potholders
- Decorative wall art
- Bags

# Chapter: 4 Techniques For Using Crochet

You would love to master a few essential crochet methods if you want to develop your fundamental crochet skills. Here are a few crochet methods that will make it simpler for you.

## 1.Crochet technique one (Front and Back Loop Single Crochet)

One of the most basic crochet stitches in single crochet. Most of the beginning stitches that people master are this one. Despite this, there are a remarkable number of items you can do with this simple crochet stitch. You may learn to operate the same stitch in only the front loop or back loop, for example. If you have done that, you will have an easy way to add rich texture to your crochet job.

It even affects the stretchiness of the fabric you are working with. You will also have a greater understanding of crochet stitch anatomy after you have mastered how to single crochet in the front and back loops. As a result, you will knit a variety of front loop and back loop stitches.

## 2. Crochet technique two (Magic Circle)

The magic circle, also known as the flexible ring or magic ring, is a fantastic place to begin a crochet project. When you want to crochet in the round but do not want a hole in the middle of the object, this is the tool to use. Folks use the magic ring to make amigurumi and circular crocheted caps, for example.

It can take a few attempts for certain people to figure out how to crochet the magic brace. It is, though, well worth knowing. When you have the feel of it, it will be one of the crochet tools you will see again and again.

## 3. Crochet technique three (Loop HDC)

Many crochet stitches have a front and back thread, as previously said. Half double crochet, on the other hand, is a little unusual since it has a third-string. It may be difficult to learn to crochet in the third loop. Also, the most accomplished crocheters neglect to learn this. However, once you plan to put it into effect, it will offer you a whole new set of choices for creating texture in your crochet work. It is a texture that can only be done by special loop work in the hdc stitch, and It is sometimes referred to as knit-like.

## 4. Crochet technique four (Crab stitch)

Reverse single crochet is another name for the crab stitch. This is the same stitch as single crochet, but it is done backward from the standard stitch. As a right-handed crocheter, you mainly work from left to right. When crocheting crab stitch, keep the job as usual but work back through the row from left to right in reverse. This results in a twisted crochet stitch that can be used as a border for a variety of crochet projects. You will already have a go-to edging if you learn it.

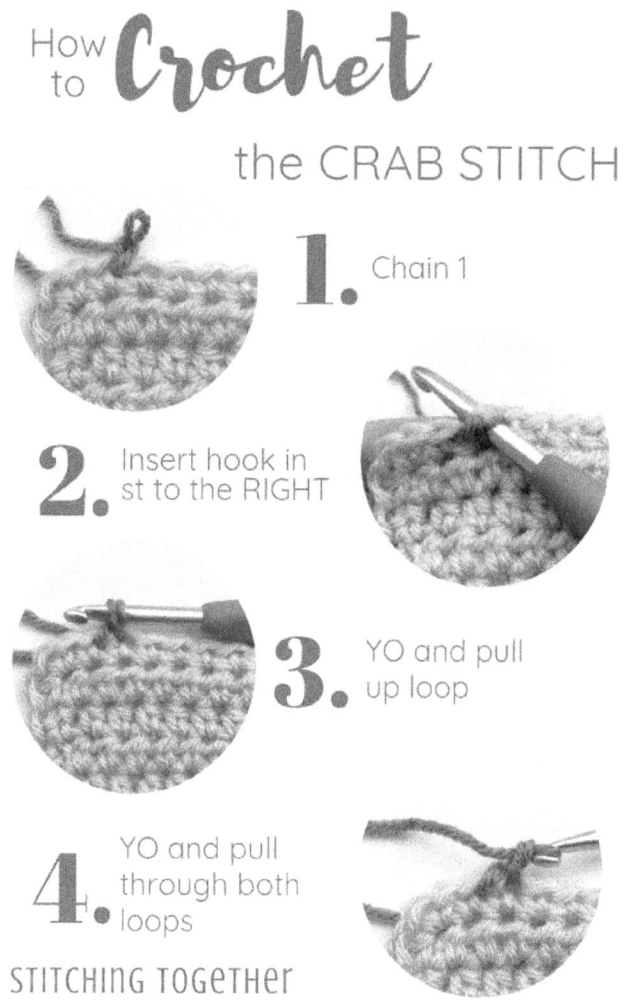

## 5. Crochet technique five (Foundation)

While foundation crochet stitches were not mentioned as one of the favorite crochet techniques, it is believed these are indeed the game-changer. It is a technique for beginning a crochet pattern with stitches rather than a string. The cloth would be more consistent as a result of this. Foundation crochet may be done in a variety of stitches.

## 6. Crochet technique six (Standing Stitches)

Standing crochet stitches, likewise, alter the game. You begin the row or round with the complete stitch rather than a chain stitch. Your stitch work would be more consistent as a result of this.

## 7. Crochet technique seven (Shells stitches)

You are able to mix the simple crochet stitches in new directions once you have mastered them. Shell stitches are a fantastic way to do this. Shell stitches are mentioned by many people as one of their favorite crochet methods. It makes sense, however, since it elevates the job while also requiring only simple crochet skills. The crochet shell stitch may be done in a variety of ways.

# Different Knitting Techniques

## 1.Knitting technique one (Combination Knitting)

There is a special method of layering the yarn on the hook when purling, and it is known as Combined Knitting. This method of knitting can help you better grasp knit and purl stitches and provide a better choice for warped knit stitches.

The provisional cast-on is a one-time use cast-on that can be unraveled later. After that, you can work on the piece in the opposite direction. This allows you to be very creative in your knitting patterns. It is often enjoyable to knit using a crochet needle.

## 2. Knitting technique two (Through the Back Loop)

Working in the back loop is certainly something you have heard about whether you crochet. Knitters may use this method as well. So, when you are just operating with one circle, you insert the needle in a separate way. It makes a twisted stitch, which brings depth and interest to your knitting.

## 3. Knitting technique three (Brioche)

Brioche knitting is a collection of similar stitch patterns. Slip stitches and yarn overs crocheted together on the previous row are included in both of them. You will need the universal brioche stitch to master all of the variants. When operating on knitting designs of your own style, you will have a couple of more choices now.

We are very interested in the methods you like using since they make crafts simpler. However, convenience is not everything.

# Specialized Crochet and knitting methods.

These crochet methods include a wide range of crochet specializations. You can start with simple stitches and work your way up to these more advanced techniques.

### 1.Method one (Tunisian Crochet)

Tunisian crochet is a good option if you are a crocheter who wants to have a taste of knitting. With just a crochet needle, you will come as nearest to knitting as possible. For this job, you will most likely need a lengthier crochet hook (also known as a Tunisian or afghan crochet hook). Loops on the hook would be placed in the same way as loops on knitting needles are held. It elevates your craft and broadens your abilities.

### 2.Method two (Crochet Colorwork)

Colorwork can be practiced in a variety of ways. Graphic patterns are readily possible. In answer to the query regarding favorite crochet and knitting techniques, mosaic crochet and tapestry crochet are the most frequently mentioned. Consider these choices if you intend to branch out of your crochet.

### 3. Method three (C2C crochet)

C2C (corner to corner crochet) is a common technique for experienced beginners. More experienced crafters will appreciate the meditative stitch repeat. Beginners, on the other hand, adore it because it incorporates familiar stitching in a creative way.

### 4. Method four (Knitting entrelac)

Entrelac may be crocheted similarly to cables. Learning Tunisian crochet entrelac is perhaps the easiest way to do it. However, there is always the possibility of going back to the beginning. Short rows are used throughout the design to produce a stunning basketweave effect.

### 5. Method five (Cables)

Knitting and crochet used to be separated by cables. There are a plethora of creative cable crocheting techniques available today. Cables were listed as one of the most common crochet and knitting techniques. However, if you want to give a really traditional look to a pattern, it is almost a must to study them for knitting.

## 6. Method six (fair isle)

Fair Isle knitting is also a form of colorwork. Fair Isle allows you to operate in just two shades, but you can add more if you choose. It is a perfect pick for typical knit pieces like this knit Christmas stocking because it has such a classic look.

## 7. Method seven (Mosaic Knitting)

Mosaic knitting is described by Knitfarious as follows:

"Mosaic knitting is a form of knitting that uses slipping stitches to produce geometric forms using two or more colors."

This is a colorwork method similar to mosaic crocheting. High-contrast patterns with a lot of pop can be produced with only two colors.

# Chapter: 5 Crochet projects, home Products and gifts

Crocheting is fast becoming a common pastime among many people. And if you are new to knitting, there are a plethora of delightfully simple designs to choose from. In reality, there are many items that you can start crocheting right now and finish by the end of the day. Here is a list of novice crochet designs for your guidance. These items will also make great presents, so if you are in a hurry and need a present, grab your crochet hooks and get ready!

Patterns for beginners are important when learning how to crochet. They are simple to learn, and you will be able to practice and perfect common stitches before going on to more difficult designs. Of course, you want to practice more than just a single Crochet because this set has designs that include a variety of stitches. They are all simple to learn, so you would not be stuck repeating the same stitch with each one. They are also ideal for those who have learned crochet and are looking for quick and simple gift ideas. Also, take a look at these designs, which will make great gifts.

## 1.Infinity Scarf

This lovely infinity scarf is easy to create as well as enjoyable to wear. It is almost foolproof, but even though you make a few mistakes, they would not appear. It is also a really simple pattern. When done, the Scarf will be between 3o to 60 inches long. If you're looking for a simple and trendy gift idea, look no further.

## 2.Tape Measure

This is a very easy crochet project. There are no raises or declines in a single round. This one would also assist you in honing your gauge, which is essential for the snail to match the tape measure. Anyone would love this simple and simple crochet present.

## 3.Crochet Baby Cardigan

If you are planning a baby shower and want to make a cute handmade present, this baby cardigan is ideal. It's a super easy little sweater to create, and based on the yarn you choose, it may be for a kid or a child. Plus, even though this is your initial crochet attempt, it will only require you an hour or two to complete.

## 4.Crochet Necklace

This task is a little different from the rest, but it's just as easy. Rather than crocheting with thread, you're crocheting the beads into this necklace. It is very beautiful and easy to create. Even if you are not a professional Crocheter, you can make it in an hour. It will be a fantastic gift for a jewelry lover.

## 5. Grocery Bag

Grocery bag can be crocheted easily. It is a best present for a crochet lover. Interesting thing is that you can crochet it in a few hours. This bag can be used as a beach bag or a normal tote.

## 6. Chain Necklace

This chain necklace is simple to crochet and can be finished in the afternoon. If you are looking for a special gift concept for a jewelry lover, this is it. The pattern notes are very clear, so there is no ambiguity, and it results in a lovely crochet necklace with interlinking strings. Use two contrasting colors and practice swapping colors.

## 7.Hot Pad

A handmade crocheted hot pad for kitchen will be a wonderful gift for any lady, and theyou only take around an hour to produce. The flower-shaped style is beautiful, and it's the ideal last minute present for somebody who has everything.

## 8.Hook Case

If you are searching for a unique surprise gift for a crochet enthusiast, this simple crochet hook cover is ideal. It would be easier to have crochet hooks handy and arranged with different parts for them. You would like to create one for yourself because this pattern is so easy. It is completed in one part and flips over like a textbook when done. You would not find a simpler crochet design anywhere.

## 9.Pencil Holder

This one is perfect for fellow crocheters or someone in need of a lovely pencil holder. The rose design is absolutely stunning, and the pattern is quite plain. The holder stays up with the assistance of a bread crumb holder, but if you choose to use stuffing instead, there is an alternative pattern. It seems to be much more difficult than it is. This could easily be completed in a single day.

## 10. Yarn Holder

If you need a gift for someone who loves crocheting as much, you'd, this easy project is ideal. It is a yarn holder that prevents the center pull yarn from being twisted when crocheting. You may even wrap your crochet project into it to prevent it from being someone who loves crocheting and needs something easy to complete in less than an hour.

## 11. Headband

This little headband makes a great crochet present for a pre-teen or teenager, plus it allows you to practice crocheting loops and double crochet stitches. It is a really basic pattern that can help you get used to dealing with chains. It also doesn't need a lot of yarn, so you can create it from scrap yarn from other ventures.

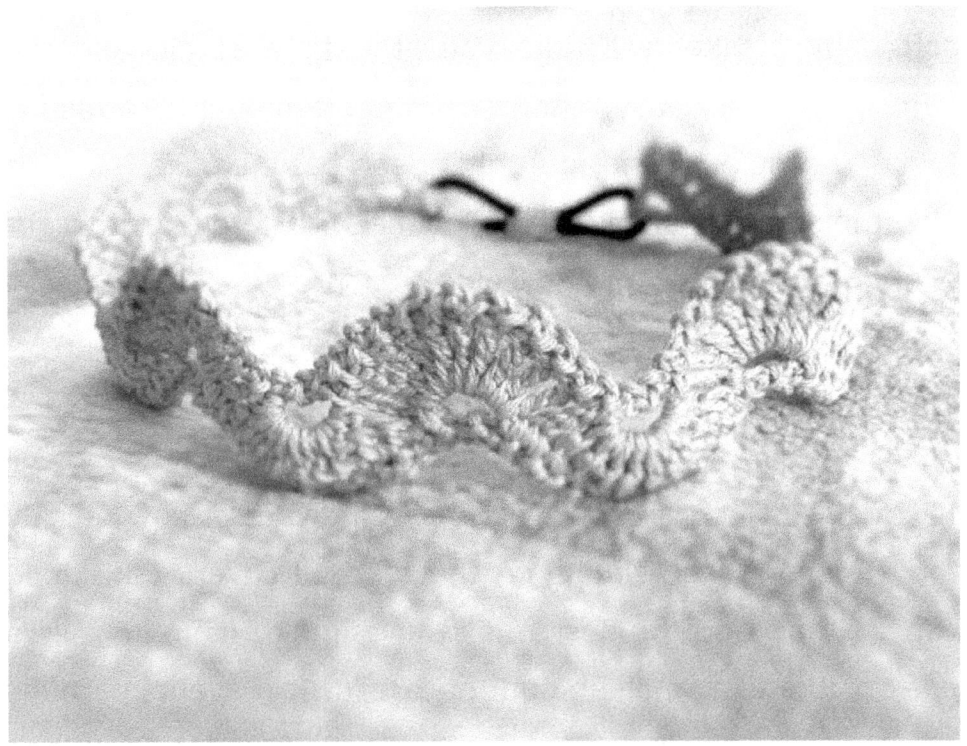

## 12.Dishcloth

Scrubbing dishes with tiny dishcloth items is a comfort, and you can even use them as a washcloth. They are probably the simplest to knit. You should create these even though you have never kept a crochet hook before since this pattern is labeled as a really simple beginner's project. You can make one of these in around 15 minutes, or whether you have an hour or so on your hands, you can make a whole package of dishcloths or washcloths as a treat.

## 13. Baby Blanket

Here is another great baby shower gift idea. Crocheting this soft baby blanket will take you little time at all, and the stitches are very easy. The pattern is often simple to follow. It has a simple repeat and only needs basic crochet stitches to complete. This blanket is an ideal choice if you want to gift everything that new moms would treasure for a long time.

## 14. Ear Bud Covers

If you are using earbuds, you are well aware of how quickly they tangle. These simple crochet earbud covers take good care of that, and the design is really simple. It just requires one stitch and a small amount of thread. It prevents earbuds from tangling and holds them secure, so they don't crack as quickly. This is a great gift idea for teenagers, and it takes less than an hour to complete.

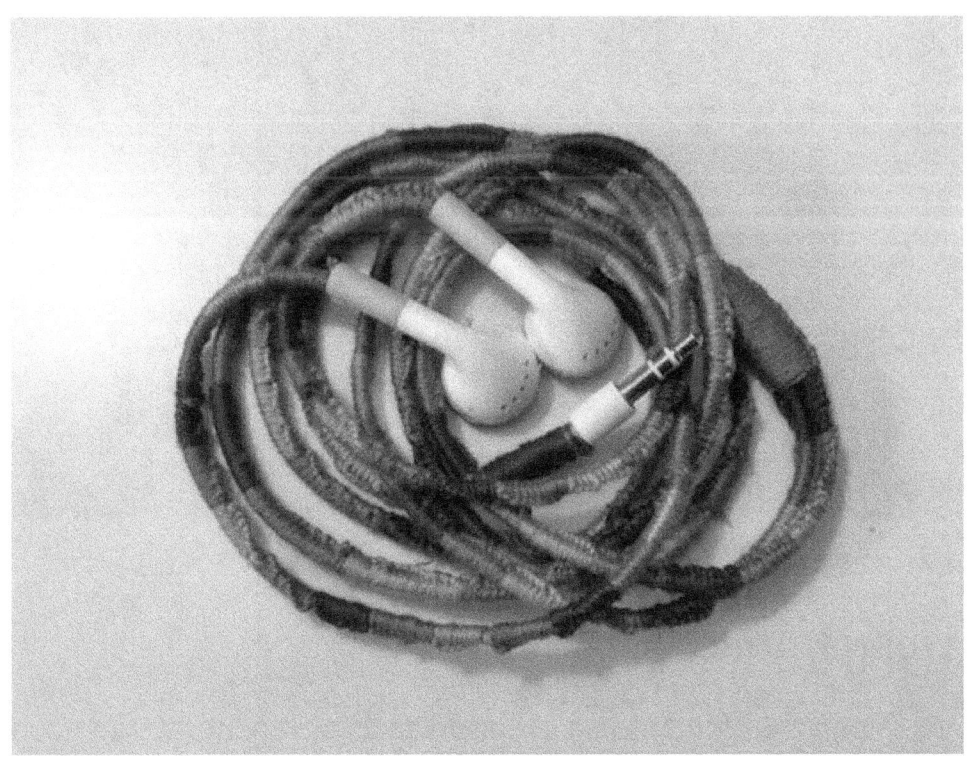

## 15. Slippers

Crocheting slippers can seem difficult, but it is not. The only time-consuming object is putting the bits together after you have crocheted them. This is the ideal project for a beginner, and it results in a lovely pair of slippers that create a fantastic gift. The pattern is simple to follow, and there are photo guides to guide you along the way. You can easily produce these in a good few hours, not counting the time it takes to put them together until they're finished.

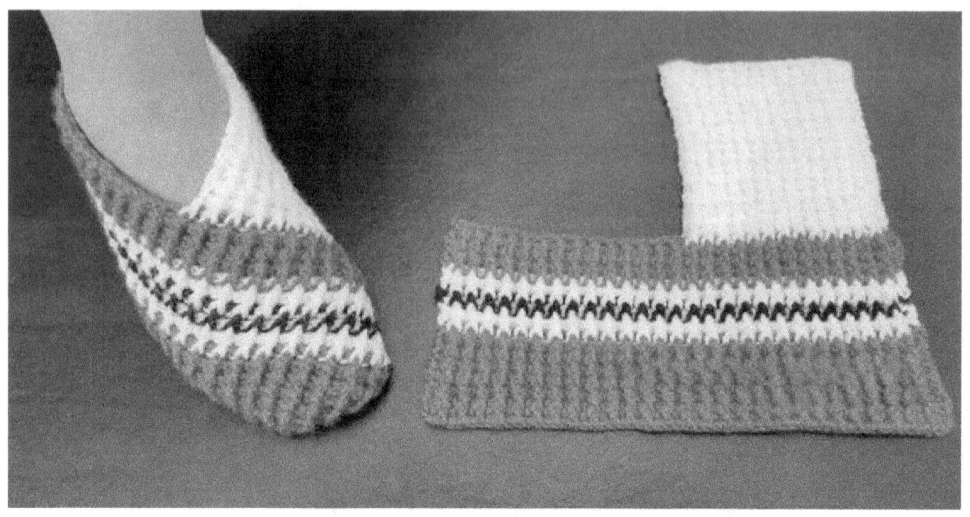

## 16. Stuff Unicorn

Hermione the Unicorn is a great project for crochet if you need a simple present for a kid. This tiny Unicorn is so simple to build and stands up three-dimensionally that every kid will be delighted to receive it – it will also make a wonderful homemade baby shower present. You'll appreciate how easy the design is to adopt, and you won't require any advanced crochet stitches. This is a great one for newcomers.

## 17. Massage Soap Saver

This crocheted soap saver includes cluster stitching on the one hand, which provides a relaxing massage when used. It is also a simple project that makes a great gift when paired with a good bar of soap.

## 18. Mug Cover

This simple and convenient crochet mug cozy is the ideal present for every coffee or tea enthusiast. Since it just uses single crochet stitches, it is ideal for beginners. This could comfortably be completed in an hour or less. It is finished with a button and a button hook, so no complex turning or stitching is needed. In the afternoon, you can comfortably make two sets.

## 19. Crochet Coasters

If you are looking for a present for someone who used to have it all, coasters are a great option. This is particularly valid if you crochet your own coasters. These little round coasters are so easy to make and take so little time to finish that you can make a matching collection of four in no time.

## 20. Stitch Markers

The crochet stitch markers are the perfect project for beginners. They will help knitters maintain track of their stitches, and they will shield knitting needles from scratching because they are crocheted. This is a really basic pattern. It is easily possible for you to make many of these in an hour.

## 21. Laptop Cover

This lovely laptop case can be crocheted in about a few hours and allows you to experiment with various yarn colors. It's an easy cover that the laptop slips into, with a good safe lock for which you'll sew a button. It's very easy, and it's a lovely case that's ideal for someone who constantly takes a laptop around with them – the comfortable wool would also help to secure the laptop.

# Chapter: 6 Crocheted Socks and Gloves and mittens

## Socks Patterns

### 1. Pattern one (Ribbed Pattern)

The ribbing on these crochet socks is what makes them so unique. They are a good match. They are incredibly nice and warm. The speckled yarn used to incorporate nuances to the pattern, though, is what sets them apart. This clever style decision makes the heels, ankles, and edging at the tip of the sock stand out.

### 2. Pattern two (free pattern)

Crochet socks are made much sweeter with a cool little ruffled edge. This is a free template that's a perfect place to start if you're new to knitting socks.

## 3. Pattern three (Nicole Cormier)

Nicole Cormier's crochet pattern is a perfect place to begin if you want to learn how to crochet socks. The toe-up style is advantageous since it allows you to try on the sock when working. This ensures you'll be able to see whether you're having the sock too large or too small. Since the design just uses simple crochet stitches, you won't require any special skills to create these adorable, warm socks.

## 4. Pattern four (Ball Hank n Skein)

This free crochet design from Ball Hank n Skein is a perfect alternative if you want to create very warm socks. These socks are produced with a size J crochet hook and thick wool weight or even heavyweight yarn. They're made to be knee-high socks that can be worn within winter boots. These socks are crafted with solo crochet and double crochet stitches, with some slight decreasing; even a novice might create them.

## 5. Pattern five (Crochet Ankle Socks)

This Nadine's Patterns lace knit style is a smooth toe-up ankle sock. It's made with a size E crochet hook and sock thread. This crochet style includes front and back post crochet stitching, quick rows, and a stitch pattern dubbed "crunch stitch" by the artist, which is also known as seed stitch.

## 6. Pattern six (Step-by-Step Crochet Socks Pattern)

This is a thorough free crochet design using fingering weight wool and a size D crochet hook to make socks. The majority of the stitches used in these socks are simple to crochet stitches. They often have the somewhat more difficult front post double crochet.

## 7. Pattern seven (Slipper Socks Pattern)

These chunky lace socks are perfect for lounging around the yard. You might, however,

pair them with shoes or wider footwear.

## 8. Pattern eight (Cabled socks Pattern)

It features crochet cables, making it a good option for people who want the appearance of knit socks but choose to crochet.

Fingering weight wool and a size C crochet hook are used in this design.

# Handwear crochet products

## 1. Fingerless Mittens

Another pair of popular fingerless mittens, this time with a cute button cuff that is very decorative. These are simple to knit and do involve a clear understanding of stockinette, knit, and purl stitches. These may be sent as presents during the holidays. They'd be perfect for someone who enjoys wearing fingerless mittens when using their tablets, and they're easy to make.

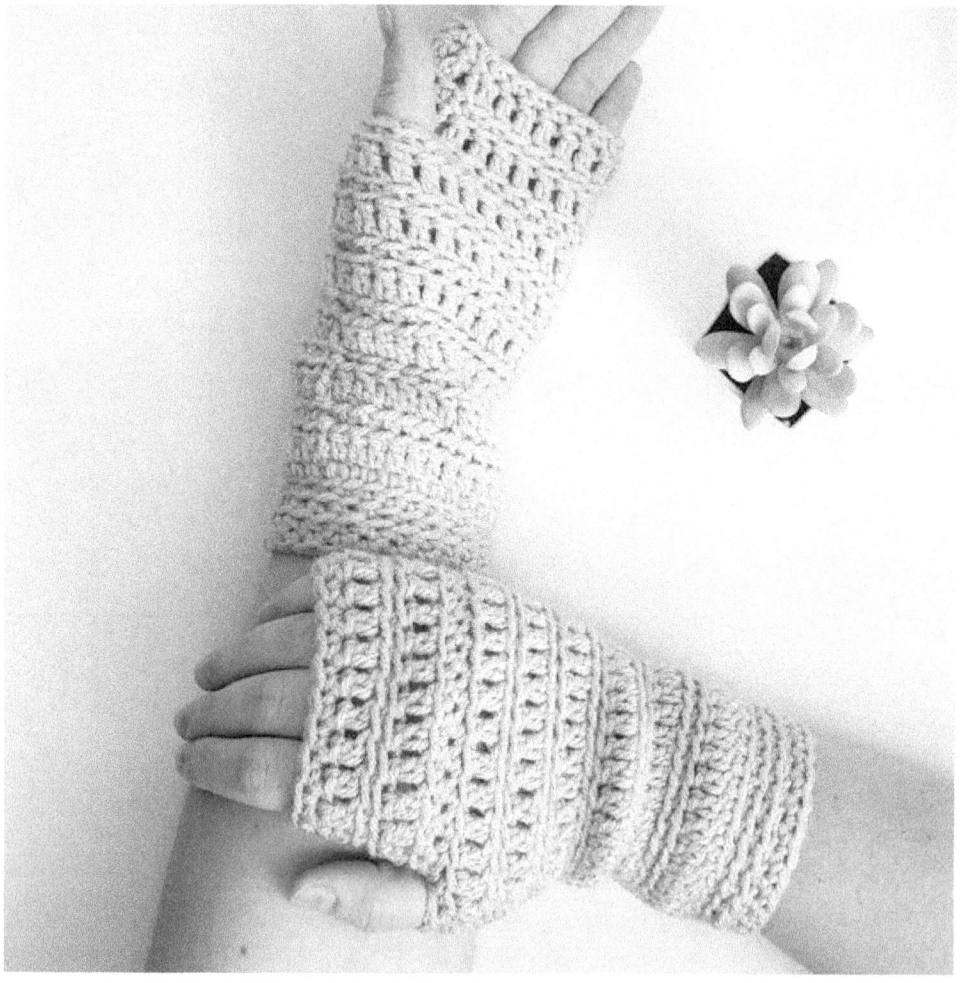

## 2.Adult Sized Mittens

The crochet mittens are for adolescents and are very simple to create. They're defined as "moderately simple" in the pattern, so even if you've never crocheted them before, you should be able to complete them.

They're still very thick, so they'll keep your hands toasty warm. You may make those for men or women; just pick a suitable yarn color and start knitting.

## 3. Button Cuff Mittens

These crocheted mittens have a great cuff style. The mittens are given a decorative look by adding a button to the wrist to hold them closed. These are simple to crochet and only need a clear understanding of stitches. And if you are new to crochet, you should be able to complete these in a couple of hours.

## 4. Fingerless Gloves

These fingerless gloves have a great style. Indeed, you can use whatever color yarn you choose, but alpaca yarn is exceptionally smooth and supple. These are often pretty simple to knit and won't take you long to complete if you have some prior knitting experience. They're ideal for bringing a touch of elegance to your comfort, and since they're fingerless, you can access your phone and other devices when wearing them.

## 5.Frozen Fingers Mittens

This crochet design can be made using any worsted weight yarn, and the colors can be

changed if desired. If you're doing this for the little girls, the use of blues will appeal to them, but you can use any color mix you want. They're simple to make and don't necessitate the use of some complex crochet stitches.

## 6.Flip-Top Mittens

When you don't need the fingers to be free, you may wear these flip-top mittens as fingerless mittens and then turn the top regularly to protect your fingers safe. Many people like the pattern because it's simple to follow and doesn't need any complex stitching. These are certainly better than going completely fingerless in the winter, particularly if your fingers get cold easily, and they warm up fast.

## 7.Hybrid Mittens

Since you have complete influence over the color of yarn used, these hybrid mittens are a stunning color. Since the tops pull back to expose your fingertips, they're also ideal for when you decide to email or use your computer. The mittens protect your fingertips warm while you don't need them uncovered. This one is really straightforward. You knit it flat and then sew the sides together.

## 8. Twine Knit Mitts

If you've done twine knitting before or not, these adorable little mittens would be a breeze to create. This is an excellent opportunity for you to discover a new method, and you will love the mitts you make. You should hope to keep these mittens for a long time after you create them because they are really sturdy.

## 9. Colorful Mittens

These vibrant mittens are made with the mitered garter stitch and look fantastic. The patterns have such a distinct appearance, and the overall design is fantastic. It's not complicated to create a mitered garter stitch rectangle. And if you've never knit before, you'll be able to complete these in no time. Change up the shades and make them suitable for both men and women.

## 10. iPhone Mitts

Another pair of mittens that are ideal for phone users is this one. They're made in a basic two-by-two ribbed design and are incredibly dense and warm! Because of the ribbed pattern's elasticity, it's suitable for a wide range of measurements. It's not difficult to change the gauge to get the exact size you need if you need anything pretty short.

## 11. Matrix Mittens

The usage of orange in some of these Matrix mittens is fantastic. And if you are new to knitting, this is a simple method to follow. When working the thumbs, you'll need to keep an eye on the yarn that "floats," but it's a simple operation. These come together easily. If you don't want orange, you can adjust the colors to anything you want.

## 12.Shark Mittens

Shark mittens are a great option for convincing children to wear gloves. Although with the various colors and precise information, the pattern is quite simple. These are going to be a hit with the kids, and they make fantastic presents for little children!

## 13. Adult Newfie Mitten

The pattern is easy, and you won't need to learn any complex stitching to complete it. To make the comparison, you'll need a pair of different shades of yarn, as well as a collection of four four-millimeter needles. This design is for adult measurements, so whenever you need to make them bigger, you should change the gauge.

## 14. Retro Crocheted Mittens

These retro-style mittens can be made in no time, and the design is suitable for both children and adults. They're made in half double crochet rounds from top to bottom. This is a perfect pattern for beginners because it's not too complex, and the mittens turn out to be really comfortable and fluffy, depending on the yarn you use. There's even a wonderful pattern on the sides that's really simple to incorporate.

## 15. Puff Crochet Mittens

Most adults will be able to wear these simple crochet mittens, and they only require two balls of yarn. Conversions and variations in rendering them of various sizes are noted in the pattern. This pattern is large enough to crochet an entire family's worth of mittens, and it's simple to follow. They warm up fast and are very strong, so they'll keep your hands toasty this winter.

## 16. Snowfall Mittens

This pattern is fantastic! With their tiny snowflakes crocheted in, these mittens are ideal for winter. They seem to be knitted, but they are simply crocheted. The pattern is simple to follow, and the dark blue colors evoke a snowfall effect, thus the name. These can be made in a matter of hours, and the design can easily be changed to fit any size requirement.

## 17. Squirrel Mittens

Squirrels are knitted straight into the adorable little mittens. The overall style is lovely, and knitting it is far simpler than you would imagine. You may make them smaller or larger as desired.

## 18. Thumbless Baby Mittens

You do not need mittens with thumbs if you have a kid. Such thumbless crocheted mittens are adorable, and the design is simple and fast to make. Since they're for little children, you won't need any yarn. They're even dense enough to hold your baby's hands warm but not so thick that they annoy him or her when they're on.

# Chapter: 7 Hats and Scarves

# Hats Designs

## Easy Crochet Hat Patterns for Beginners

From simple one-stitch beanies to chunky knit hats, you'll find a hat that you'll enjoy crocheting below.

## 1.Design one (Simple Crochet Beanie)

This hat is made with Lion Brand Wool-Ease Thick & Fast, which means it knits up quickly due to the ultra-bulky six yarn.

## 2.Design two (Leigh Textured Crochet Hat)

This type of Crochet Hat can be made with Lion Brand Jeans yarn which is awesome!

This is a simple hat to make for a complete beginner. Since it only uses one stitch, the pom striped hat crochet design is ideal for beginners. This beanie is easy to create.

## 3.Design three (simple Crochet Beanie)

This beginner-friendly crochet beanie pattern uses just one cake of yarn and is simple to produce. When the yarn changes color, you won't have to weave in different ends! Caron Cupcake yarn is used in this pattern, which is perfect for working projects and looks really good in almost every pattern.

# Scarf styles

Crochet scarves may be as simple or as difficult as you want them to be. This set of crochet patterns includes novice patterns as well as more complex patterns for more experienced crocheters. Choose from the basic patterns if you're only discovering the method to make Scarf through Crochet. Prepare to make something you'll be proud of!

## 1.Style one (Striped Neck Scarf)

It's a plain square scarf with a dotted design in black and white. Its shape allows you to conveniently loop it around your neck or use it as a fashionable hair accessory. You'll be able to create a lot of crochet scarves with this design.

## 2.Style two (Infinity Scarf)

This Crochet Infinity Scarf is crocheted with a lot of texture and can be paired with almost everything! It's made with a simple stitch double crochet on the front post. For the most part, that's what this Scarf has to do! If you have the feel of it, it's a pretty simple stitch to master, and the texture it produces is incredible!

## 3.Style three (Textured Scarf)

This beginner crochet pattern for an infinity scarf is ideal. This is perfect if you want to create something soft and cuddly. This Scarf is incredibly squishy, fluffy, and somewhat textured.

## 4.Style four (Chunky Crochet Scarf)

Using three strands of yarn and a large crochet hook, understand what to do to crochet a chunky scarf pattern. This Scarf is simple to produce and can be customized in a variety of ways. It's a lot of fun to practice how to fashion a scarf this way.

## 5.Style five (Super Scarf)

This scarf crochet design is easy to create and goes with about every outfit that requires a little something special. It's both lengthy and broad enough for it to be worn in a variety of ways. Try it bundled around both shoulders, tucked under a scarf, or layered over a similar t-shirt to stay comfortable. If you're just getting started, this is one of the simple patterns to follow.

## 6.Style six (Ribbed Scarf)

With variegated yarns that shift color quickly, the Easy Crochet Scarf looks way nicer. It's a basic design in which each single crochet stitch is crocheted in the back loop. This Scarf is suitable for both men and women. The pattern would look great on both men and women.

## 7.Style seven (The Boyfriend Scarf)

The delicate features in the Scarf make it appear polished and distinguished. One of the most traditional forms of scarves. The precise ribbed stitch is used in the Scarf for additional texture. It's also a decent duration, ideal for wrapping up in. The yarn preference, however, is the feature that truly distinguishes this Scarf.

## 8.Style eight (Simple Scarf)

Crochet has many of the characteristics of a great hobby. It's cheap, entertaining, and a perfect way to unwind. The loop stitch, as well as the half double crochet, are the only stitches included throughout this basic crochet scarf design, making it ideal for beginners.

## 9.Style nine (Double Crochet Scarf)

This simple double scarf crochet design is suitable for both beginners and specialized crocheters. Using this Scarf to practice working double crochet, knowing how to keep a straight point, and having even stress if you're new to crochet.

## 10.Style eleven (Reeva Scarf)

This is one of the simplest free crochet scarf designs to make; everyone can do it. Making stunning crochet designs would not necessitate the skills of a crazy scientist. When the simple crochet stitches are merged, they usually result in a rather attractive design. You will not be disappointed if you try this Scarf.

## 11.Style eleven (Basic Scarf)

This is the easiest crochet design. With this crochet scarf pattern, you'll just need to know two crochet stitches: the loop stitch and the single crochet stitch. This is about the simplest crochet scarf template you could ask for, making it an excellent beginner crochet accessory pattern. It is the perfect crochet accessory pattern for beginners. It's also written for people who don't have extensive experience reading crochet patterns.

# Chapter: 8 Crochet Bags

You can Crochet a lot of unique and fascinating bags and tote bags. Below are some of the most beautiful and enchanting bag designs. You must choose the crochet hooks and demonstrate your inner crocheting abilities and expertise. So, let's have a peek at the fascinating list below and get some ideas. It is hoped that the following stunning and trendy creations will motivate you.

## 1.Bag pattern one (Market Bag Pattern)

This lovely market crochet bag is absolutely gorgeous and will bring a touch of glitz to your appearance. Flowers, beach staples, veggies, slices of elegant cheese, and slices of bread and tons of loaves of bread. This Bag cries to be packed with pretty stuff and basic yet exquisite ingredients. This crochet market bag was made of thick textured white, grey, and golden wool.

## 2.Bag pattern two (Yarn Bag Pattern)

This Bag is large enough to hold anything you need. It's made of silky wool string and features genuine leather for a special look. This wool crochet bag has a really sleek appearance. It comes with a top handle which can also be worn as a shoulder pocket. Detailed cloth lining and a pocket to keep your phone.

## 3.Bag pattern three (Tote Pattern)

It's around the right time to also offer you a crocheted tote bag. The Bag is easy to make; just bear in mind that crocheting with paper twine needs more power than crocheting with cotton or linen twine. This Bag also makes a perfect Christmas gift, and you can change the size by increasing or reducing the number of rows in the design.

## 4.Bag pattern four (Free Crochet Bag Pattern)

Super cool yarn straps are fixed with rivets on this crocheted beach case. This beautiful beach bag is made with cotton yarn in two different shades, a crochet thread and stitch markers. Because of its similarity to the ocean, the dark blue and white paint combination has enhanced the appeal of this Beach pack.

## 5. Bag pattern five (Granny Bag Pattern)

This crochet bag is made up of beautiful sunburst granny squares made of Cleckheaton California 100 percent wool in Mauve Glow and a 4mm hook.

Twelve crochet squares, hooked together in two sets of 32 columns and rows, base color cotton and acrylic thread in the same color, lining fabric, and wooden handles are needed for this Bag.

## 6.Bag pattern six (Summer Bag Pattern)

This big summer crochet bag is influenced by the Caribbean's sandy beaches. This lovely tote features cheerful stitches and striping and is ideal for carrying blankets, picnic lunches, or your new farmers' market finds. This lovely summer crochet bag was made with thick yarn in pink, grey, and light pink colors.

## 7.Bag pattern seven (Market Tote Pattern)

Your quest for the ideal Bag has come to an end! This Bag is perfect for visits to the grocery store or long beach days. It's big enough to hold anything you need; however, it folds up for fast storage and transportation. It is simple to look for and disinfect since it is made of lightweight, sturdy cotton.

## 8.Bag pattern eight (Market Bag Pattern)

Introducing a crochet big market bag with a unique shape and a plethora of useful features. Unlike several other crochet packs, this one totally opens up as it lies flat, allowing you to bring your fruits and vegetables in without having to cram them into a little hole at the end. When you lift the pack, it coils around your belongings and transports them away. Consider individuals who hold something in front of them with their aprons or a kid carrying something in front of them with their shirt.

## 9.Bag pattern nine (Fancy Bag Pattern)

The Fancy Marketplace Crochet Bag is unlike any other crochet bag pattern you've seen. This market bag stands out from the other free bag templates thanks to its elaborate style. Any time you go to the grocery store, you'll undoubtedly get several compliments. The best part about this crocheted Bag is that it takes just a few hours to complete. It's not very often that you walk across a stunning bag that's also simple to create.

## 10.Bag pattern ten (Masa Bag Pattern)

It's a straightforward crochet bag. Nothing wild, only a big triangle of single crochet or half double crochet to complete the project. It's cool because of the way it's folded to produce an Origami impact.

## 11.Bag pattern eleven (Bag of Colors Pattern)

This charming bucket bag is made of cotton and features bright zigzag patterns on the exterior. The Bag's strap is long and drapes around the back. It has an unlined interior that can be used to store a range of objects and accessories.

## 12.Bag pattern twelve (Mesh Bag Pattern)

Pattern for a crocheted mesh market purse. There's a ton of free crochet mesh bag designs to choose from! Mesh bags are clean and airy, and they can be rendered compact enough to slip into your handbag and carry shopping with you. As you take them out, they stretch to accommodate your food!

## 13. Bag pattern thirteen (Dot's Bag Pattern)

Are you looking for a gift purse, a knitting or sewing bag, or a lunch bag? For any cause, lingerie, shoe, make-up, scratch, pin, or small Bag? Sew a charming Drawstring Ditty Bag! This simple unlined bag tutorial includes a durable fake bag underside that you can create to ensure that your little Bag maintains its cute design.

## 14. Bag pattern fourteen (The Dragon Egg Bag Pattern)

It's an easy design, and you'll just need to know how to thread, half-double Crochet, Double Crochet, and slip stitch to complete it. It may seem amazing, but it is incredibly user-friendly. Use a hook size or two smaller than the yarn's recommended hook size; the label for this Lion's Brand Vanna's Choice (in Cranberry) suggests a J hook for the measure, but a G hook was used to make the egg denser, heavier, and less prone to lose dice.

## 15. Bag pattern fifteen (Raffia Messenger Bag)

In the spring and summer, the natural feel of raffia is appealing. The roundness of the handmade backdrop gives it a cute shape. With the curvature in the basic style that saved decoration, the shoulder back has an adorable shape. The ZIP files that the cavity provides are useful.

## 16. Bag pattern sixteen (Kitty Bag Pattern)

The foundation of this adorable small Tapestry Crochet Kitty Pouch is crocheted first, then the edges spiral outward to shape the sides, so the width of the core is not increased. This adorable tapestry crochet kitty bag can be made with blue and white paint variations.

## 17. Bag pattern seventeen (Raffia Bag Pattern)

The interior of palm tree leaves may be drained of a straw-like material. The fibers can only be contained in a certain palm tree species that grows in abundance throughout Sub-Saharan Africa. The artisans use a needle and thread to knit the raffia fibers into a variety of forms, patterns, and items that are stunning in actual raffia shades or when hand-dyed.

## 18. Bag pattern eighteen (Fat Bag Pattern)

Anyone who decided to create anything for the spring might do so. It is a plain bucket crocheted bag design with bamboo handles. The stitches are all beginner-friendly.

## 19. Bag pattern nineteen (Market Bag Pattern)

This crochet purse design is the most basic of all the purse patterns available. The Single Skein Market Bag is easy to create, even for beginners. Because of the double crochet stitch, this Bag can end up being very spacious and ideal for shopping.

## 20. Bag pattern twenty (Lacy Bag Pattern)

This free crochet tote bag is ideal for a market handbag or a day at the pool. Crochet totes, also known as farmers' market bags, are becoming increasingly common among fashionable women. Crochet tote bag is handcrafted and suitable for every design or event. This lovely, orange-colored market bag can be made of polyester thread, yarn, rope chain, polyester yarn, chunky thread, and bulky yarn.

## 21. Bag pattern twenty-one (Hobo Bag Pattern)

Crocheted hobo bag with a multicolor pattern that looks really interesting. This pattern creates an elegant bag with matching front and backsides by combining chain and single Crochet. This crocheted hobo bag can be made with high-quality yarn in white, blue, and brown colors.

## Conclusion

It is so fascinating that no device can crochet. Any of the Crochet you've ever seen is handcrafted, even store-bought crochet. Crocheters will crochet at a fast pace! For this cause, certain people like crocheting. And if a crochet machine existed, crochet is always easy enough to be enjoyable to do by hand. Hand spinning, by the way, is indeed a lot of fun right after the invention of knitting machines in 1589. For a variety of causes, robots cannot fully substitute it. This book is a salute to a lifelong love that has gifted countless people with the beautiful art of crochet.

The hand knitting band "Crochet" has a plethora of possibilities for bringing creativity to the design knit garment industry. Women, especially in rural areas, will contribute their enormous ability to the yarn crafting industry's reputation. This will have a tremendous incentive to use local expertise while still engaging them in the enrichment of the clothing knit industry. The execution of this goal should begin at the market level, where the potential must be produced alongside the machines used to make fashion knit garments. Through their successful participation in this campaign, designers will put a lot of credit on this. Designers could make the scope easier when integrating efforts with the business. As a result, the potential of incorporating the skill of those people from our community into the art of crocheting would be created.

Crocheting for charity is another enjoyable hobby for crocheters. Crocheted pieces, especially caps, scarves, and mittens, are appreciated by hundreds of charities. Crochet is a simple craft to pick up. Anyone should learn to crochet; there are several good beginner books available, such as this one. The Chain Stitch is the first stitch to master after having the Skein of yarn and a crochet needle. Learn how to make the Single Crochet Stitch, Slip Stitch, Half Double Crochet, and Double Crochet stitches next. We can create a lot of stuff with these simple stitches. We may follow a trend or create our own. Have a wonderful time doing this fantastic hobby!

www.ingramcontent.com/pod-product-compliance
Lightning Source LLC
Chambersburg PA
CBHW081414080526
44589CB00016B/2537